THE YEAR IN TENNIS 1997

DAVIS CUP® by NEC

THE YEAR IN TENNIS 1997

TEXT BY CHRISTOPHER CLAREY

THE INTERNATIONAL TENNIS FEDERATION

UNIVERSE

First published in
the United States of America
in 1997
by **Universe Publishing**
A Division of Rizzoli International
Publications, Inc.
300 Park Avenue South
New York, NY 10010

98 99 00 01 / 10 9 8 7 6 5 4 3 2 1

Printed in England

Designed by Derek Ungless

CONTENTS

President's message

I have many responsibilities as President of the ITF, but one that I also regard as a privilege is to witness the magnificent competition that is the Davis Cup. At least four times each year, I am able to watch the best players in the world compete in Davis Cup, knowing that playing for your country has its special pressures balanced by enormous personal rewards. All you need to do to find the heart of the competition is to look at the photographs, taken by some of the most talented photographers in the sport. Just look at the faces in triumph and in defeat. See the joy of Jonas Björkman in Sweden's moment of glory, the pride that the American team displayed in their victory laps after defeating Australia, the despair on the face of Adrian Voinea as Romania saw their lead disappear against the Netherlands. Emotions, highs and lows, are what Davis Cup is all about.

Davis Cup continues to grow, with 131 nations entered for the 1998 competition. It prospers because—to be blunt—it works. Over the years, changes have been made to improve the competition but never to alter its spirit. Davis Cup strikes a chord in the players and in the spectators, both live and on television. It means something to play for your country; it means something to win the Davis Cup and everyone knows that.

We hope you enjoy the 1997 Davis Cup Yearbook. The author, Christopher Clarey, has done an enormous amount of original research and has brought to life this year's competition. Our photographers from all over the world have brought their special insight to this year's Davis Cup.

It was a great year for the champions, Sweden, and the finalists from the United States, but we start all over again in 1998. We hope you will join us and witness Davis Cup in person. From my seat, I can tell you honestly that you will love it.

Brian Tobin
President
International Tennis Federation

Foreword

It is a great honor for me to be asked to write the foreword for the Davis Cup Yearbook.

Among the highlights of my Davis Cup career was twice playing a fifth rubber when the outcome of a tie depended on my match being won. The first time was against Germany's Carl-Uwe Steeb and was especially rewarding as my win meant that USA advanced to the 1991 Davis Cup Final. Then, a year later, I defeated Karel Novacek in the fifth rubber when USA defeated Czechoslovakia in the World Group quarterfinals. I was honored to have been part of the American team's success, particularly when we went on to win the 1992 trophy.

Moving on to the 1997 Davis Cup, I was disappointed that I was not able to be there for the semifinals and Final, but with Pete and Michael playing so well, Captain Tom Gullikson made the right choice. Like every loyal American, I followed my team with interest all year and felt their disappointment at losing in the Final.

I congratulate the Swedish team on a great victory. I also congratulate and commiserate with my teammates from the United States. They did a great job defeating a hot Australian team to get to the Final and had some bad luck with Pete's injury. I know what it feels like to be part of a team that fights all year only to lose in the Final. It happened to me against France in 1991. It's awful.

Davis Cup has been an important part of my career since I first played for the United States a few weeks before my eighteenth birthday in April 1988. I remember my excitement and my pride at being part of the U.S. team that defeated Peru in Lima in the American Zone semis and then, later that year, defeated Argentina in Buenos Aires to put the United States back into the World Group.

I have experienced firsthand the highs and lows of Davis Cup. I take great pride in knowing that my name is carved on the trophy with the greats of the game. I look forward to getting the opportunity to play for the United States next year. Nothing would please me more than bringing home another Davis Cup title. And, while I treasure my Grand Slam titles, Davis Cup and my Olympic gold medal are so special because I won them as part of a United States team, and I love playing for my country.

Andre Agassi

The Davis Cup:
Shelter from the storm

"STRANGE YEAR," SAID PETE SAMPRAS as 1997 drew to a close.

Strange indeed. Though Sampras remained number one throughout the season, the hierarchy beneath his designer sneakers was rumbling and shifting on what seemed to be a weekly basis.

It was a year for bolts from the blue: Brazilian Gustavo Kuerten, who had never won a tournament on the main circuit swept through the draw, ignoring all logic and pressure, to win hearts, minds and the French Open. It was a year for journeymen to become leading men: Patrick Rafter, Jonas Björkman and Greg Rusedski all soared into the top five. It was a year for the serve-and-volley style to rise up roaring from the grave; a year for seeds to be planted and rarely germinate.

"It's getting like golf," said Patrice Clerc, the French Open tournament director. "I think when a Grand Slam begins these days, there are truly twenty to thirty men who believe in their hearts that they have a chance of getting to the Final."

Strange indeed. But Davis Cup proved essentially immune to the larger trend. Yes, there were upsets and upheavals: Italy's defeat of Spain and subsequent implosion being the most salient example. But there was nothing that left the mouth agape, as there had been in 1996 when the Czechs knocked off an under-strength American team in the quarterfinals and the French beat the Swedes in what was arguably the most dramatic Final in Davis Cup's lengthy and distinguished history.

Drama and tennis make fine bedfellows, but in truth, a return to the status quo was exactly what this competition needed. It has been buffeted in the distant and recent past by lack of commitment from top players, and though the French were certainly appealing and theatrical champions in 1996, their low-ranked performers were off-Broadway caliber, and, as any impresario can tell you, allowing understudies to creep into too many leading roles will eventually dim a production's aura.

And so for those who value Davis Cup, there was something rather comforting about the later rounds in 1997, when the game's rising and established stars were reassuringly present. The semifinal between the United States and Australia featured the world's top three singles players and its top doubles team. The Final between the United States and Sweden featured three of the world's top four singles players (although not for long) and an explosive doubles team in Björkman and Nicklas Kulti that certainly has the potential to be the world's best.

Of the players who finished the year ranked in the top ten, only Sergi Bruguera did not play Davis Cup in 1997, and that was because nobody asked. The only member of the year-end top 20 who declined to play throughout the year was Richard Krajicek, and even he expressed a desire to return to the Dutch team in 1998, when he plans to prune his schedule considerably.

The schedule, of course, remains the bane of Davis Cup, and it remains to be seen how the new stars, such as Rusedski, who have surfaced in the wide wake of the retired Stefan Edberg and Michael Stich and semi-retired Boris Becker, will view their sport's preeminent team competition as the demands on their time and bodies increase exponentially.

Such demands were not an issue in 1899 when a twenty-year-old Harvard student from St. Louis

The founder: in 1899 Dwight Filley Davis started a competition that has grown to be one of the sporting world's most influential.

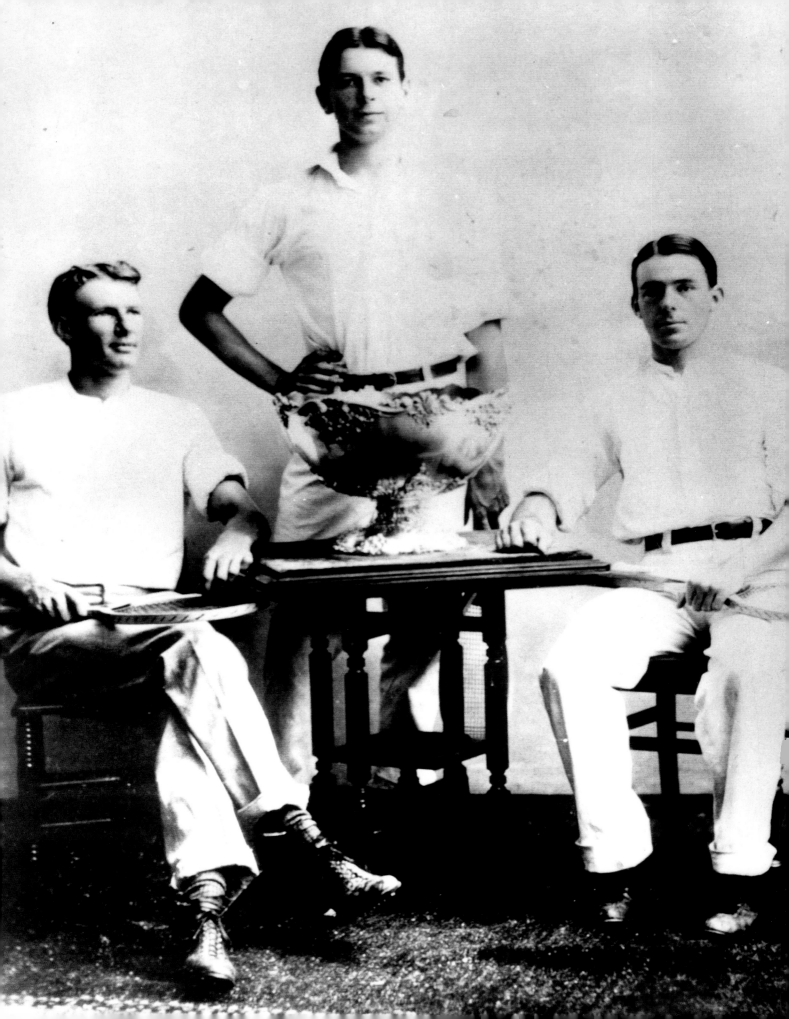

Beginnings. The British were the first to take up the challenge from the U.S.

The 1900 Davis Cup-winning team from the United States, opposite, consisted of Malcolm Whitman, Dwight Davis and Holcombe Ward. Great Britain first took the Cup in 1903 with the Doherty brothers: Reginald, above left, and Laurie, right.

Tony Wilding, Australasia's ace New Zealander, kept the Cup down under from 1907 to 1911 and again in 1914 when the competition was halted by the outset of World War I.

named Dwight Filley Davis asked a Boston silversmith to shape 217 troy ounces of sterling silver into a punchbowl. As Australian journalist and author Alan Trengove informs us in his authoritative history, *The Story of the Davis Cup*, Davis had just completed the first tennis tour of the United States along with three other future Harvard alumni—Holcombe Ward, Malcolm Whitman and Beals Wright—and he was in an expansive and expansionist frame of mind.

Tennis, at least in its outdoor guise, was a new game, and opportunities to compete internationally were exceedingly rare instead of enervatingly common. Davis, brimming with youthful enthusiasm and precocious vision, wanted his shimmering trophy to serve as the prize for an international challenge event. He had to settle for bi-national at first, because in 1900, when the Davis Cup was launched, the only challengers were the British Isles. When the British arrived at Longwood Cricket Club in Boston in the midst of a typically steamy August, they arrived without their two finest players, Laurie and Reginald Doherty, and were promptly bushwhacked by Davis and the Americans.

The British were defeated by the climate, the length of the grass, the consistency of the balls and the strange and wondrous effects produced by the new and elusive "American twist" serve, which at times left them as defenseless as Aztecs in the face of Spanish musket fire. The globalization of tennis had begun, and though the Davis Cup was not contested in 1901 because the Doherty brothers again declined to play and Britain had no desire to risk another humiliation, the Dohertys would soon decide that this fledgling competition was worthy of their attention and perspiration.

Surprisingly, the Americans beat them and Britain again in 1902, but the following year at Longwood, the Dohertys restored pride to the nation that invented modern tennis and so many other modern games by defeating the former colonies 4-1. The British would hold the Cup for the next four years, thereby establishing Davis Cup's dynastic bent.

Wizards and musketeers

The Challenge Round system encouraged such dynasties because it allowed the reigning champion to wait imperiously for the other challengers to eliminate each other and then host the Final: fresh and on its own terms.

There would be Australasia with Tony Wilding and Norman "The Wizard" Brookes from 1907 to 1911 and again in 1914, just before a dark and destructive four-year hiatus caused by World War I. There would be the United States and Big Bill Tilden from 1920 to 1926; France and its charismatic four *mousquetaires*—Jean Borotra, René Lacoste, Henri Cochet and doubles specialist Jacques Brugnon—from 1927 to 1932. There would be Great Britain and Fred Perry from 1933 to 1936.

Nowhere did the Cup mean more than in Australia, where it became a rallying point for a new, melting-pot nation in search of an identity. The isolated continent joined the Davis Cup fray in 1905. At the time, Australians and New Zealanders were members of the same team: hence the now-archaic moniker of "Australasia." But the Australasians were no match for that other melting-pot nation, the United States, losing 5-0 in 1905 in the final round of the qualifying round at the Queen's Club in London.

They were quick learners, however. The following year, Australasia lost to the Americans 3-2, and in 1907, they were the 3-2 winners as New Zealand's dashing Wilding and Australia's calculating left-hander Brookes—both the sons of first-generation English immigrants—did the heavy lifting and carried off the punchbowl to the Southern Hemisphere: thereby providing logistical nightmares to challengers for years to come.

The good news was that the Cup's signature rivalry had begun in earnest and for much of the mid-twentieth century, the Australians and Americans took turns battling seasickness, jetlag and each other in an attempt to earn bragging and champagne-sipping rights. From 1938 to 1959, the two nations met in the Davis Cup Final every year the event was contested and from 1937 to 1973, they were the only two nations to win. Most of the men who starred on those teams remain very familiar, even now: Don Budge, Bobby Riggs, Jack Kramer, Pancho Gonzalez, Tony Trabert, Vic Seixas, Dennis Ralston, Chuck McKinley, Arthur Ashe and Stan Smith for the United States; Adrian Quist, Frank Sedgman, Lew Hoad, Ken Rosewall, Neale Fraser, Fred Stolle, Rod Laver, Roy Emerson and John Newcombe for the Australians, whose ringmaster was their captain-journalist-drill sergeant Harry Hopman, whose tight grip on his players would be impossible to re-create in the late 1990s.

But bicameral rule was not necessarily positive for the Cup as a whole, and after the Open Era began in 1968, the competition was soon suffering in earnest because the Davis Cup governing body decided to exclude such contract professionals as Rosewall, Laver and Newcombe. The decision was not made out of ignorance—it was an attempt to limit the influence of promoters—but it turned out to be a blunder as the Grand Slam and other open events took flight and the Cup quickly lost altitude.

Better players; bitter problems

Reform was the response. In 1972, the anachronistic Challenge Round was consigned to its rightful place in the past, and in 1973, the contract pros were invited to take their rightful place in the present. Newcombe and Laver soon showed the bureaucrats what they had been missing by trouncing the Americans, 5-0, in the Final in Cleveland. But that crushing and emotional victory surprisingly did not mark the end of the troubled era for the competition that the idealistic Dwight Davis had hoped would promote better understanding among nations.

In 1974, South Africa and India both reached the Final for the first time, but India refused to play because of South Africa's apartheid policies, and the Davis Cup soon had its first and only walkover champion. The following year, it had another new champion, Sweden, in considerably happier circumstances, as the unflappable Björn Borg won all three of his rubbers against Jan Kodes and Czechoslovakia. But the Cup, even for optimists, was still half empty and the continuing presence of South Africa and apartheid-ruled Rhodesia continued to create tension and diplomatic incidents. In 1976, the United States, France and Britain actually announced their resignation from the competition because of the creeping politicization. That crisis was averted, but some of the game's top players, particularly Jimmy Connors, remained more difficult to convince of Davis Cup's intrinsic worth.

John McEnroe, who had played a year of university team tennis at Stanford, did not need convincing. After the temperamental American assumed supremacy in the men's game after Borg's eclipse, Davis Cup's darkest years were behind it. NEC's title sponsorship provided financial stability and, for the first time, prize money in 1981, the same year the elite World Group was launched teaming the sixteen strongest tennis nations with the other nations in zonal groups striving for promotion.

The World Group format, combined with the increasing depth in men's tennis and the increasing demands on the top players, has put an end to the dynastic era, but it has not done much to democratize the elite. Since 1981, only five nations have won Davis Cups: the USA, Australia, Sweden, France and Germany, which won its first titles in 1988 and 1989 with the iconic Becker playing singles and doubles and then won again in 1993 with Stich, Becker's longtime and less iconic rival, working overtime.

Europeans. From 1927 to 1936, the Cup was dominated by *les mousquetaires* and Fred Perry.

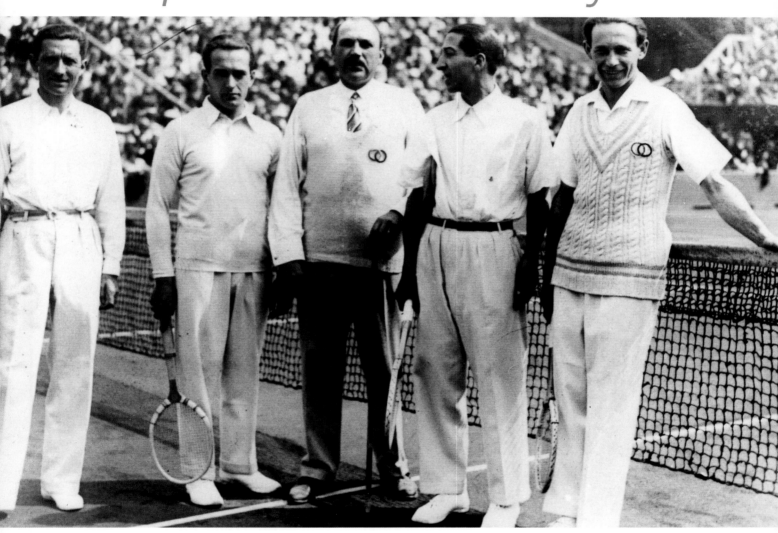

Opposite: Great Britain's greatest, Fred Perry. Above: the French team, commonly known as the four mousquetaires *flank the director of Roland Garros Stadium (center). From left to right, Jacques Brugnon, Henri Cochet, René Lacoste and Jean Borotra.*

Team USA wins its twenty-fifth Davis Cup title in 1978. From left to right: Bob Lutz, Stan Smith, Captain Tony Trabert, John McEnroe and Brad Gilbert.

But Davis Cup has become markedly more democratized at the lower levels. This competition might have begun as the United States versus the British Isles, but it has evolved into the world's largest annual team sporting event with nations playing in five different divisions ranging from the World Group with its household names to the freshly minted, twenty-three-team Group IV with its household-sized nations and obscure republics.

Atlas required

Since 1981, the number of nations involved has soared from 51 to 127. Only the teams in the top three groups now use the traditional Cup format in which two nations play best-of-five-set rubbers over three days. In Groups III and IV, the fifty-five nations entered in 1997 played round-robin in their respective zones. Each tie lasts only one day and consists of two best-of-three-set singles and a doubles match. The ITF essentially underwrites Groups III and IV, paying travel, lodging and food expenses for five members of each team and covering a significant chunk of the host nation's organizational expenses. Total cost for spreading the game? Approximately one million dollars per year. "There was some question whether we should just allow nations to take part or find some kind of qualification standard," said Davis Cup director Thomas Hallberg. "But in the end it was felt that once a nation became a full member of the ITF, they should be able to take part in Davis Cup and be part of the family."

Without family planning, Group II had to be added in 1988, Group III in 1992 and Group IV in 1997. For the moment, Hallberg insists there is no thought of giving birth to Group V, but with the post–Cold War fad for independence and with four more nations becoming full ITF members in 1998, bringing the Davis Cup total to 131, perhaps Hallberg had best avoid any rash predictions.

"I don't think a lot of the players realize what's going on down there," said Newcombe, now Australia's captain. "Egypt playing Uruguay, if they're playing in Egypt, is a huge thing in Egypt. They sing the national anthem. They get passionate, and that's what happens every year in all these matches. People don't understand. They lose the forest for the trees. Some of the top players think of the little picture and are only concerned with themselves. The Davis Cup is so much bigger than the top players."

In principle, that is true, but it is also true that the game's stars are the ones who generate the interest and revenue to support Davis Cup's rapidly broadening base. Hence, the tinkering continues. There have been discussions about reducing the World Group matches to best-of-three sets and more serious discussions about reducing the World Group from sixteen to fourteen nations and granting the previous year's finalists a first-round bye and early-season breather in the midst of an absurdly cluttered schedule. But the thornier problem for the ITF remains the question of dates.

"I happen to think the dates are one of the most important things in attracting the best players," said ITF president Brian Tobin.

The top players generally agree that the current season is too long, and if they don't now, their aching bodies will soon convince them. If the men's tour does indeed stick to its plan of restructuring its calendar in 2000, Davis Cup must ensure it does not get lost further in the reshuffle. For the moment, the Cup dates, often the week following major events, are less than ideal, but for anybody who sat in the rambunctious, sold-out stands in Gothenburg for the 1997 Final or on the warm, cement bleachers in Gaborone, Botswana, for the first Group IV match in history, the ideal is clearly still alive.

Most players still relish representing their nation, and most tennis fans still relish watching them do it.

Boris Becker, opposite, began playing Davis Cup in 1985 after his first Wimbledon win. John McEnroe, above, was a willing participant and always ready to answer his country's call.

ROUND ONE

Noah's ark goes down under

IT WAS FEBRUARY IN SYDNEY, and Arnaud Boetsch once again dropped to his knees after winning a Davis Cup singles match on a Sunday. But the difference between this victory celebration and the one Boetsch launched in Malmö barely two months before was as wide as the Australian continent.

This was a mock celebration, an ironic, utterly self-conscious act at the end of a dead rubber. France, the reigning champion, had fallen to earth, or more accurately to turf, in the very first round.

The French team's 4-1 defeat on grass at the hands of the resurgent Australians was no shock. In truth, it was considerably more logical than their run to the title the previous year without the benefit of a single player ranked in the top 20. Just as in 1992, when the French went down to defeat against the Swiss in the first round after winning the Cup so unforgettably against the Americans, *la grande fête* turned out to be very brief.

"For a team like ours to win, it must seize every opportunity," said France's captain and ringleader, Yannick Noah, on the eve of the tie. "We're not going to produce exploits every time. Believe me, I'm not trying to prepare myself for defeat, but I do remind myself that winning the Davis Cup with the team we had last year was a serious exploit."

In Sydney, the exploits were left to the home team, so hungry for success after spending all of 1996 subsisting on the comparatively meager fare of Group One. It was the first time in history the Australians had not been part of the World Group, and the Australian team leaders, captain John Newcombe and coach Tony Roche, had every intention of making it the last.

In February, their players' rankings—with the exception of the world's number-one doubles team, Todd Woodbridge and Mark Woodforde—were no more intimidating than the French team's had been the year before. Just like Noah, Newcombe and Roche consider Davis Cup an opportunity to form bonds that permit a team to equal more than the sum of its parts. Also like Noah, Newcombe and Roche believe fighting the good fight for one's nation can transform a player, lifting him onto a higher plane than he can hopefully sustain on his own.

Schmaltz? Psychobabble? Anyone in need of proof need only consider what happened to Patrick Rafter both during and after the tie's opening rubber against France's number one, Cedric Pioline.

Rafter had spent much of the previous two years in his own lonely version of the outback, struggling with overnight celebrity, overbearing expectations and wrist and shoulder injuries. After breaking into the top 20 in 1994, he struck bottom in the spring of 1996 when his ranking dropped to 89, and when he walked onto the historic center court at White City—site of so many Australian heroics in the past—he was still only 64th.

This was the first home singles match of Rafter's heretofore unexceptional Cup career, and after losing the first two sets, it did not appear that his luck was ready to change. After blowing a 5-1, two-break lead and losing the second set in a tiebreaker, he walked over glumly, sat down next to Newcombe and muttered, "Sorry, that's the biggest choke I've ever seen."

That was when Newcombe decided it was time to turn up the volume and turn on the colorful language.

Australia's not-so-secret weapons: the Woodies. Todd Woodbridge and Mark Woodforde showed why they are ranked number one in the world in doubles by winning the decisive point over the holders—France—in Sydney. Preceding pages: Moya-mania in his home of Mallorca inspired a Spanish victory over Germany in the opening round.

The Aussies left Noah and his team completely adrift and waiting for the qualifying ties.

Captain Yannick Noah's French team sailed into Sydney, above, as the defending champions but foundered against Australia in the first round. Right: raising the rafters: home court advantage as Australian fans cheer on their side at historic White City.

"He just had his head down and his tail between his legs," Newcombe said. "So I figured it was time for us to get down in the gutter with a little bit of gutter talk. So we had a one-way heart to heart with a few very choice adjectives. The bottom line at the end was that, 'This is a war of attrition, and it's going to be one point at a time and if it's going to take three more hours, that's how long we're going to be out here.' But I told him, 'The only way you're going to be able to do it is if you dig down inside your guts and find something you didn't know was there.'"

Such in-your-face pep talks were nothing new for Newcombe, a famously intense competitor during his remarkable career as a player. In his first tie as captain in 1994, after Woodforde and Woodbridge lost the first two sets against Russia's Yevgeny Kafelnikov and Andrei Olhovskiy, Newcombe delivered an equally impassioned speech at the changeover.

"Newk just exploded," Woodforde said with a grin. "'You guys are the bloody Wimbledon champions. What on earth do you think you're doing? This is disgusting! Get your tails up. Don't even sit here!' He was letting us know that we were playing for our country and what we were producing wasn't good enough. He was dead right, and we clawed our way back in, although we ended up losing in five sets."

This time, it was Rafter's turn to do the clawing—even if, as he admitted later, he didn't know what the word "attrition" meant—and this time, there would be no five-set defeat.

It was a matchup between two of the finest all-around athletes on the men's circuit. With his leaping ability and grace, Pioline could easily have been a volleyball star like his mother, who once played on Romania's national team. With his exceptional reflexes and innate fluidity, Rafter could certainly have been a fine cricketer—or less appealing to an Australian—a fine running back.

Mark Woodforde (top) and his big leftie serve took out France's Arnaud Boetsch in the second singles to the delight of the crowd at Sydney's White City.

Pioline walked on court sporting a legionnaires-style cap of the sort Ivan Lendl used to favor when he braved the heat of an Australian summer. He had missed the Australian Open with back pain and had not played an official match since blowing a two-set lead against Sweden's Thomas Enqvist on the final day of the 1996 Davis Cup Final. That loss had burnished his reputation as a player who lacks the conviction to succeed in long, close matches. But despite his fourteen double faults against Rafter, the self-contained Frenchman, who would reach the Wimbledon final on grass later in the year, did not throw away this nail-biter as he has thrown away others. Instead, Rafter wrested it from his grasp, lifting his game, improving his returns and covering the net like a goalkeeper.

When Rafter, who had never rallied to win from a two-set deficit, evened the match at two sets apiece, Newcombe exchanged glances with Noah.

"It was the first time we had caught each other's eye," Newcombe said. "We smiled at each other as if to say that this is what Davis Cup is all about: two people locked in combat."

The combat turned for good at 3-3 in the fifth set when Rafter broke Pioline with a gorgeous backhand pass down the line. Pioline would save three match points before Rafter hit his last well-placed first serve of the afternoon into the Frenchman's body. By the time the return hit the net after four hours and fifteen minutes of plot twists, the Davis Cup had its first great match of 1997, and the Australians a huge psychological edge.

Rafter had more of an edge than anyone and would end up winning the U.S. Open seven months later. "They say you have the best and worst moments of your career in Davis Cup," he said. "This is one of the best moments of my life."

"That match turned Pat's whole career and his whole life around," Newcombe would say after watching Rafter hoist the trophy at Flushing Meadows in September.

In all, the Australians would need only three matches to turn the tie against the French into an exhibition. After Rafter's resurrection, the thirty-one-year-old Woodforde—a surprise choice in singles with his 1-7 record in live rubbers—played an excellent grasscourt match to defeat Boetsch in straight sets. The following day, the redhead from Adelaide played three more fine sets with Woodbridge to clinch it for the Aussies against the strong French doubles pair of Guy Forget and Guillaume Raoux.

It all made for a whirlwind visit for Christian Bimes, the president of the French Tennis Federation. Very recently reelected, despite the open opposition of Noah and most of the top French players, Bimes arrived in Sydney on the morning of the first singles matches and flew home to France immediately after the doubles, skipping the traditional Saturday night dinner and an awkward moment with his defeated team. To his credit, Bimes apparently does not hold grudges because, within weeks, he had acceded to the French women's players request and named Noah captain of the Fed Cup team: a decision that would quickly lead to some replacement silver for the lost Davis Cup.

A tale of two psyches

While the combustible French struggled to reconcile external and internal forces, the Australians were the portrait of harmony. In 1994, when Newcombe and Roche, best friends and one of the best doubles teams in history, acceded to their posts after the retirement of Neale Fraser and a contentious succession battle, they were already facing skeptics.

"The first thing you have to understand is that for almost fifty years, Australia had only had two Davis Cup captains, Harry Hopman and Neale Fraser, and they'd never had in that whole period of time a captain and coach," Newcombe said. "But Tony and I started talking about it, and we felt there was a need here for a new type of thing to be evolved. It didn't meet with a huge reception from Tennis Australia because change is not readily accepted amongst sporting bodies. It was sort of a huge fight actually, and right from the beginning after we were chosen, Tony and I were each approached by Tennis Australia to break away from one another and do it by ourselves. But it's impossible to split two blokes like Tony and myself who have been together since 1964. We believed this was the right thing to do, and I think we've been proven correct now.

"It's a different world today and the players are so much individuals. They have their own private coaches and trainers and managers and people advising them. It really requires two of us to get this job done."

They did not get the job done immediately. In their debut, the team lost in the first round in Russia and then lost again in the first round in 1995 in South Africa before losing the relegation match in Hungary, 3-2, in September. That unprecedented defeat prompted a Hungarian reporter to ask Newcombe if he would resign. Newcombe politely told him to mind his own nation's business, but there were certainly some Australians who were entertaining similar thoughts.

Fifteen months later, however, the Aussies had succeeded in reacquiring some of their hallmark edge.

"I think what we've created is the team spirit of all for one and one for all, which was what existed when Tony and I were playing," Newcombe said. "These boys know we're not doing this because we want their fame or their money. We're doing this because we care about tennis in our country and about them as people. If we didn't think they were nice blokes, we have a lot of other things we could be doing that would pay us a hell of a lot more money."

It spoke well of Newcombe and Roche's evolving stewardship that, even in the absence of their top

Two very promising juniors

"It was 1954 and the Australians were hosting the U.S. in the Davis Cup Final. They had built temporary stands at White City way up into the sky. I was way up in one stand, a ten-year-old with his dad. In another stand was nine-year-old Tony Roche with his dad. I was from Sydney. Tony was from a small country town several hundred miles away, where his dad was a local butcher. We were both dreaming that day that we might be able to represent our country out on that court, and we eventually did. And when we played against France, here we were both back at White City and in charge of the team. What you had were two guys who had gone full circle."

John Newcombe

two singles players—the ailing Mark Philippoussis and Jason Stoltenberg—the Australians still cruised into the second round. But then the Aussies were hardly alone. Such absences (due to injuries, illnesses, real or imagined scheduling problems, and in the case of Boris Becker, aversion to Spanish clay) were the rule, not the exception, throughout the eight first-round matchups in the World Group.

Playing with fire

The United States traveled to Brazil without world number one Pete Sampras or world number two Michael Chang; Germany traveled to Spain without Becker or Michael Stich; the Dutch to Romania without reigning Wimbledon champion Richard Krajicek and the Russians to South Africa without reigning French Open champion Yevgeny Kafelnikov, who had playfully thrown a right jab at a punching bag in Melbourne just prior to the Australian Open and ended up breaking his playing hand in two places.

The Germans and Russians would end up reaping the whirlwind: the Germans falling 4-1 to fast-rising Carlos Moya and the Spaniards on Moya's picturesque home island of Mallorca; the Russians falling 3-1 to world number eight Wayne Ferreira and the South Africans in the steamy coastal city of Durban, where on-court temperatures soared above fifty degrees centigrade on day one, inspiring a local journalist to write that it made "a sauna feel like a freezer."

But the Americans and Dutch would survive without their main men in uniform. Of the two teams who would end up facing each other in the quarterfinals, the Dutch did the most intense flirting with disaster.

Even without Krajicek, who was recovering from arthroscopic knee surgery to repair a slight tear in his meniscus, the Dutch were clear favorites on paper against the Romanians, who were making their return to the World Group after a twelve-year absence. The two Dutch singles players—Jan Siemerink and Paul Haarhuis—were experienced Davis Cuppers ranked 21 and 27 respectively. The Romanians—Adrian Voinea and Andrei Pavel—were ranked 45 and 131, and the Dutch also had one of the finest doubles teams of this decade in Haarhuis and Jacco Eltingh.

But paper is often a poor material to rely on when predicting the outcome of a Davis Cup tie, and after the first day, the Romanians were up 2-0 after Voinea had disposed of Haarhuis in four sets and Pavel of Siemerink in four sets.

"When you play for your country, it doesn't matter the ranking of your opponent," Pavel said.

Voinea's and Pavel's relationships with their country are complex. Both were born in 1974 and grew up under the hard-line regime of dictator Nicolae Ceaucescu without the same opportunities as their tennis-playing peers in the West. Chances to compete internationally were rare because visas were difficult to procure, and many older talented players never realized their potential or dreams. In December 1989, when Pavel was fifteen, several talented Romanian juniors, including Irina Spirlea and Ruxandra Dragomir, were preparing to fly to Miami to compete in the prestigious Orange Bowl junior tournament. Then came word that Nadia Comaneci, Romania's Olympic gymnastics hero, had escaped from the country and been granted refugee status in the United States.

The exit visas were cancelled. One month later, Ceaucescu was deposed and executed, and the borders were flung open. Voinea had already made his way to Italy; Pavel soon landed in Germany, but both now play Davis Cup for their homeland.

Neither played in Saturday's doubles, however. Instead, Romania's captain, the former Davis Cup

Jan Siemerink (top) outlasted a shell-shocked Adrian Voinea (bottom) in five long sets in the fourth rubber to even the tie at 2-2. The Netherlands completed the comeback from 0-2 down against Romania when Paul Haarhuis defeated Andrei Pavel in the fifth and decisive match.

player Florin Segarceanu, chose the relatively unseasoned team of Razvan Sabau and Ion Moldovan. Although the first set went to a tiebreak, the difference in experience and polish soon became apparent as Haarhuis and Eltingh put Holland on the scoreboard with a straight-set victory.

That set the stage for a pleasantly memorable Sunday for the Dutch and a painfully memorable one for the Romanians. The first reverse singles between Voinea and Siemerink lasted five sets and four hours and twenty-one minutes. In the fourth-set tiebreaker, Voinea had three match points. Winning any of them would have put Romania into the second round, but the relentlessly aggressive Siemerink saved the first with a good backhand volley that forced Voinea to miss a backhand pass wide. He saved the second when Voinea overhit a forehand long. He saved the last with another superb backhand volley that landed in the corner for a winner and leveled the tiebreaker score at 8-8.

Two points later, Siemerink evened the match and after breaking Voinea in the ninth game, he soon evened the tie at 2-2 by closing out a 7-6 (8-6), 5-7, 6-7 (3-7), 7-6 (10-8), 6-4 victory that was even more exhausting to play than it is to read. The fifth rubber was merely denouement as Haarhuis beat a visibly deflated Pavel in straight sets to make Holland the latest on an increasingly lengthy list of teams to erase a 2-0 deficit.

From 1981, when the World Group was established, until 1988, no nation clambered out of that hole to win. But in the last decade, with increasing depth in the men's game, seven teams have done it. The Brazilians did not become the eighth when they hosted the Americans in the city of Ribeirão Prêto in the highlands of São Paulo State. But they were a great deal closer than they probably realized.

Into the sauna with Guga

Brazil had earned the right to play in the 1997 World Group in a controversial and thoroughly unprecedented manner. In September 1996, while hosting Thomas Muster and the Austrians in a qualifying match in the city of São Paulo, Muster walked off the court during the doubles and refused to finish the fifth set, claiming that someone in the crowd was blinding him by using a mirror to reflect sunlight into his eyes. He said other fans were making noise during points, insulting and spitting at him. Security, in his mind, was insufficient for him to continue.

The Austrians forfeited that match to give Brazil a 2-1 lead and then angrily decided to forfeit the last two singles matches, which gave Brazil a place among the Davis Cup elite. Though the Austrians later protested and Muster appeared in London to plead his case before the Davis Cup Committee, his $8,000 fine—clearly more symbolic than onerous to a modern-day plutocrat baseliner—was upheld. Brazil, whose home crowds had drawn protests (but no sanctions) in 1992 and 1993 from the visiting Germans and Italians, were considered by the committee to have, in this case, fulfilled their security obligations and were not given a warning. In the committee's view, Muster had overreacted.

Warning or no warning, American captain Tom Gullikson and his cobbled-together team led by Jim Courier flew to Brazil in a wary frame of mind, well aware that they would have to deal with a rambunctious crowd, slow red clay, high temperatures and moderately high altitude of approximately one thousand feet. As it turned out, they would also have to deal with the future French Open champion, the gifted, rail-thin and extra-terrestrially fit Gustavo Kuerten, who had been one of Muster's doubles opponents during that hot-tempered match in September.

As usual, the Americans were at less than full strength as their top players elected to husband their resources for more individualistic endeavors. Even the United States Tennis Association's decision to significantly increase its payments to players did not stem the tide of evasion.

Sampras, who declined but promised to play if the Americans reached the semifinals, had not made himself available since the 1995 Davis Cup Final against Russia. Chang had agreed to play in only one tie since the 1990 Final against Australia. Todd Martin was injured, and Andre Agassi, mired in one of his periodic bouts of complacency, had committed to play and then showed up noticeably out of shape and with a slight ankle injury for the pre-tie training camp in Miami, Florida.

"It was clear he hadn't hit too much," Gullikson said. "And it soon became clear he wasn't going to be ready to play."

Gullikson scrambled and secured the services of MaliVai Washington, a dangerous player who is normally less dangerous on clay. Washington would do Gullikson and himself proud in the opening rubber, beating Kuerten in four tight sets. But he would pay an exorbitant price for his third Davis Cup singles victory, injuring his knee in the third-set tiebreaker. Though he would finish the match on adrenaline, the injury would keep him out of action for the remainder of the year.

Courier, who had cramped in practice earlier that week because of the extreme heat and humidity, was the next American into the gauntlet, and he would need five sets to defeat the Argentinian-born baseliner Fernando Meligeni. When Meligeni won the fourth set, hundreds of cardboard fans that had been handed out to the fans came raining down onto the clay in celebration. There was a lengthy delay to clean up the debris, but again no warning was issued.

"The crowd was in my face, in my kitchen a little bit," Courier said. "They're in the back of the court and just yelling things like, 'You're not getting out of here alive. We're going to kill you. We're going to kill your mother.' They were yelling that in English. Whatever they were saying in Portuguese I was lucky enough to not understand. Sometimes it's good you don't speak the language. It was vengeful stuff. There was no sportingness about it."

What made Courier particularly sensitive to the taunting was that his mother, Linda, had flown in from Florida to attend the match.

"Of the seven away matches I've done in Davis Cup, that was by far the worst treatment we got from the fans," Gullikson said. "We just basically had to block it all out and not respond to it and not be affected by it. I thought our players did a phenomenal job of that. I can easily see how Muster walked off the court now, and I have no doubt he was abused down there, as well."

It should be made clear that in Davis Cup, one player's or captain's earful is another's serenade. Though Courier had played in Mexico in his disappointing Cup debut, Gullikson had never experienced the nonstop commotion created by a South American crowd.

"In my opinion, you can never have enough passion in Davis Cup or any tennis match," said Kuerten, who has never understood why Muster stomped off in a huff. "In Brazil, the crowd is lively and colorful. This is what tennis needs if you ask me."

Whether the crowd was colorful or crass, the Americans still had a comfortable 2-0 lead heading into Saturday's doubles match between Richey Reneberg and Alex O'Brien and Kuerten and Jaime Oncins. With Reneberg's experience and dependability and O'Brien's explosiveness, Gullikson felt his team was a solid favorite, but when Reneberg, a new father, played like someone who had recently experienced too many sleepless nights, the Brazilians ended up with a surprising straight-set victory, and Courier ended up with the tricky task of handling the twenty-year-old Kuerten and his highly subjective fans.

What made it even trickier was that the injured Washington was now unavailable. That meant

Road warrior

"This year, I've probably had more people come up to me and thank me for playing Davis Cup than people coming up and asking me for anything else. Playing American tournaments, I've really felt it for the first time this year: people really appreciating it. And I think it's because they see other guys not playing and they see me playing. They see basically that you screw up your schedule the first half of the year and throw away a chance to make points for your ranking to do something like this. It's important to me now. I think that if I look back on my career to this point, I think a lot about Davis Cup. It is such a part of the history of tennis, and if you want to be a part of that history, it's nice to have your name on the silver bowl. And I love hearing them say 'Game United States.' I've played a lot of junior team competitions, and I've always loved that."

Jim Courier

Courier won the critical fourth rubber, silencing the cries of Guga! Guga! Guga!

Carnival in Brazil: sunny skies and spirited spectators greeted the Americans in Ribeirão Prêto, left. Former Roland Garros champion Jim Courier outlasted the soon-to-be French champion Gustavo Kuerten of Brazil to put the United States in the quarterfinals.

Almost at the top of the world, icy Lulea was the site of Sweden's opening-round victory over Switzerland. Thomas Enqvist, then Sweden's number one, anchored his team to victory against Switzerland, middle: "I love to play Davis Cup and I love to play for Sweden. We have a wonderful team spirit." A five-set victory over Magnus Larsson and his crimson shoes were the only bright moments for Swiss number one Marc Rosset, bottom, in the opening round against Sweden.

that if Courier lost, Davis Cup rookie Alex O'Brien would have to face Meligeni and the crowd in the decisive rubber.

"That just kind of put a little extra whammy on the situation," Courier said. "Davis Cup is a huge learning curve. So I felt quite a bit of pressure going out there and trying to get that match taken care of."

Gullikson had scouted Kuerten in Australia, and though the Brazilian was considered a better hardcourter than claycourter by many at that stage, Gullikson recognized Kuerten's ability and, more specifically, his potent down-the-line backhand: a shot that gives Courier trouble because of his propensity for leaving his stronger forehand wing wide open.

"We were all respectful of Kuerten," Gullikson said. "He could easily have beaten Mal. He had a lot of chances. He just didn't take his chances."

He could easily have beaten Courier as well. The former world number one had missed two months of action near the end of 1996 with a knee injury and despite his French Open titles in 1991 and 1992, he had not won a claycourt title in four years. But Courier, after a flickering start, has come to value Davis Cup more than some of his contemporaries and on Sunday against Kuerten, he played like it mattered immensely.

He won the first two sets with relative ease, 6-3, 6-2, but Kuerten lifted his game to win the third 7-5 on a double fault by Courier. While the American was beginning to tire in the heat, the Brazilian appeared to be getting stronger, sprinting to his seat on changeovers, exhorting and communing with the crowd as it chanted "Guga, Guga, Guga." In the sixth game of the fourth set, Courier felt a cramp in his calf and immediately realized that this set had better be the last. He started taking greater risks and shortening points, but Kuerten held firm as the quality of play soared and the match careened into a tiebreaker.

Kuerten saved the first match point at 6-5 and the second at 8-7.

"What I remember most about all the match points was I don't remember anything that was going on with the crowd," Courier said. "It was pandemonium around me I'm sure, but it was complete calm inside me. I knew that I was about to lock up with cramps, so I couldn't afford to waste any energy thinking about anything else."

On the third match point at 9-8, Courier hit a first serve on the back of the line that Kuerten somehow swiped back across the net. It landed short, and Courier ran forward to hit the sort of forehand he has hit for a winner tens of thousands of times. But as he bent his knees and exploded upward toward the ball, both his legs cramped. His shot struck the tape and fell back.

"Luckily my legs relaxed when I came down," he said. "But I knew that if I lost the set, I was not going to be able to finish the match. They were going to have to carry me out of there."

Kuerten, who said he never noticed Courier was suffering, would save the fourth match point at 10-9 with a forehand winner, and then it was Courier's turn to save a second set point at 10-11 with a serve to Kuerten's body. Two points later, Kuerten hit a second serve and moved forward to hit a backhand after a relatively weak return. This time, the Brazilian was the one who knocked a makeable short ball into the net.

The crowd finally fell silent. Courier had won the tiebreaker 13-11; the Americans had won the tie. Courier was too exhausted to emote. He simply raised his arms wearily in the air and waited for the red, white and blue wave of Gullikson and his teammates to wash over him.

"It was all slow motion," Courier said. "Relief, joy, anger at the crowd. I went over and hugged my mom and just was yelling in her ear how much I wanted to get out of the country. I've never wanted to beat a country so badly in my life."

When Courier finally made it to the locker room, he would need immediate intravenuous treatment to stop the cramping that had begun again in his legs and was creeping into his lower back.

"At least I waited until he got done with his I.V. before I asked him to play in the second round," Gullikson said. "I figured Jim had certainly earned the spot if he wanted it."

The iceman cometh—the Czech man goeth

The other teams who earned spots in the second round were Sweden, Italy and the Czech Republic. The Swedes, in their first match of the post–Stefan Edberg era, chose to promote tennis near the Arctic Circle by hosting the Swiss in the small, very northerly city of Lulea on the Gulf of Bothnia. With temperatures outside hovering around minus 30 degrees centigrade, Marc Rosset gave the visitors the first rubber by defeating Magnus Larsson 13-11 in the fifth set, but that Herculean indoor effort only left him less energy for the mammoth tasks to follow. After playing five more sets and losing in doubles on Saturday, Thomas Enqvist was simply too fresh and strong for the towering Rosset in Sunday's decisive fourth rubber, winning 6-3, 6-2, 3-6, 6-2. The Swedes, with Edberg cheering from the stands, would go on to win 4-1.

Considerably farther south, the Italians chose to host the Mexicans outdoors at the Foro Italico, home of red clay and monumental Mussolini-era statuary. Though they looked more like the Italian ski team as they watched in their hefty jackets from the chilly sidelines, the 4-1 victory was straightforward. The same could not be said for the Czech Republic's 3-2 victory over India and its leader, Leander Paes, on a slow indoor claycourt in Pribram.

When Paes and partner Mahesh Bhupathi defeated Petr Korda and Martin Damm on Saturday, the Indians led 2-1, but on the final day Korda held off the 122nd-ranked Paes—exponentially more dangerous when playing for his country—in four sets and then announced that he was retiring from Davis Cup play at age twenty-nine. Jiri Novak then gave him an excellent parting gift by defeating Bhupathi 6-1, 6-4, 6-3 in the final rubber.

And so the quarterfinal matchups were set: USA-Netherlands, Australia-Czech Republic, Italy-Spain and Sweden-South Africa. The losers were left to ponder what might have been and what already had been, in some cases so very recently.

"I would have loved to have had a little more time to digest our victory," said a wistful Guy Forget. "I have the impression that we played the Final in Malmö just two weeks ago and that we are still the champions and that the event we just lost in was a different event altogether."

Patrick Rafter

OTHER PLAYERS have experienced it before him, including his American measuring stick Andre Agassi. But this was Patrick Rafter's year to close the yawning gap between his fame at home and his accomplishments between the lines.

He closed it by reaching the semis of the French Open and winning the U.S. Open, beating Agassi along the way. It began in February with Davis Cup and with the same men—John Newcombe and Tony Roche—who had selected him to play singles in their very first tie as head of the Australian team three years before.

"Those guys have so much to offer and so much to tell you," Rafter said.

Newcombe and Roche had long believed that Rafter had the makings of a Grand Slam singles champion, and at age twenty-four, he proved them right and himself wrong.

"I always dreamed about it," Rafter said, "But I honestly never thought I'd win one."

Rafter's grasp exceeded his reach in 1997 for a number of reasons. He improved his volleys; put more sting and spin on his already fine serve and achieved more consistency from the baseline. But for Newcombe, the key ingredient was less tangible.

"Greater self belief," Newcombe said. "His low periods over the preceding eighteen months had been due to injury and also the things that happen to players when they get instant celebrity status. They have a hard time dealing with that, and even apart from the injuries, Pat wasn't doing himself justice on the court. There wasn't this total commitment and belief in what his destiny was. Tony and I felt that once Pat got this belief, he'd be fine. And I think that happened during the match against Cedric Pioline. You can take it into tennis and all walks of life, but usually a turning point happens, and it's a dramatic period. From then on, people go from strength to strength."

Rafter does not hail from an affluent background. The seventh of nine children, he was born in the copper mining town of Mount Isa in the Australian state of Queensland and can remember running toward the local dirt tennis courts full of hope at age five.

"There used to be a wall underneath our garage," he said. "And I'd hit against the wall and then run down the road to see if there was anybody to hit with." Rafter gravitated toward tennis because his three older brothers played, and after getting an early taste of rugby in his family's backyard—"I managed to break a few bones"—tennis seemed like a better idea. Through the years, as his family made sacrifices to nurture his talent, Rafter slowly, tantalizingly developed into the next great hope of a nervous tennis nation that had seen its torrent of champions reduced to a trickle named Pat Cash and then to nothing.

The fact that Rafter was handsome ("Meet me after Rafter" read the banners) and relatively well-mannered certainly didn't discourage the hype, which reached its peak in the fourth round of the 1995 Australian Open, when he faced Agassi. But the Las Vegan, in one of his periodic phases where tennis mattered greatly, pounded Rafter 6-3, 6-4, 6-0 and accelerated what Rafter already considered a downward spiral. In September of that year, Rafter felt so disoriented that he actually declined to represent Australia when it traveled to Hungary for what would prove a futile attempt to avoid relegation from the Davis Cup World Group.

"I let my team down," he said. "That's the worst memory of my career."

Rafter missed most of the first half of the 1996 season with wrist and ankle problems but put his time out of the limelight—now focusing intensely on his strapping friend and doubles partner Mark Philippoussis—to good use. And this time, when the victories started coming and the probing questions followed, he was ready: "I know who my friends are now. It's all got to be careful," he said. "That's the learning curve I've gone through over the years. I'm just going to try to stay the same person I am."

That person plans on playing Davis Cup until Newcombe and Roche stop calling: "Winning the U.S. Open is pretty bloody good, but playing for your country is the best. It's a shame some of the Americans don't have the same feeling. It's a national pride thing. That's the way I see it. I'm one of the first with my hand up, and I will continue to be that way."

The new world order

YOU LEARN A GREAT DEAL of tennis trivia at the bottom of the Davis Cup pecking order.

You learn that Botswana's playing captain went to Choate; that Liechtenstein's is too young to vote; that Iceland's number one is a UCLA freshman and that Togo's has a left-handed serve that could make many a Bruin varsity stalwart quake in his free-list sneakers.

You learn that Sudan's best play on grass (Nile permitting) and that Madagascar's best prefer the clay in France (residence permits permitting). You learn that the finest emerging players in Uganda hail from the euphonious city of Jinja and that you and many of your weekend-warrior friends with Africa-sized hitches in their swings are good enough to play Davis Cup right this very minute for Djibouti.

You learn more consequential things, too, when you spend a week loitering at a Euro/African Zone Group IV match far below the equator and even farther from the tightly wound, bottom-baseline world of the ATP Tour.

You learn that countries with border disputes get along better with racquets instead of rifles in their hands. You learn that John Kasule, a Ugandan coach, is toiling earnestly to rebuild tennis interest in a country that is rebuilding and that a round and remarkable woman named Euphemia Tlhapane has spent the last thirty years introducing southern African children to tennis's maddening delights and just so happens to be the foster sister of South African hero Oliver Tambo, the former president of the ANC.

Above all, you learn that despite the manic racquet-tinkering and collective hand-wringing of recent years, tennis and its body language are—surprise, surprise—increasingly universal: that certain Icelanders scream in anguish after a botched volley just like certain Long Islanders; that certain Togolese pump their fists after an ace just like certain Taiwanese; and that Djiboutians don't like getting double-bageled any more than you or your friends with those big hitches. It just happens to Djiboutians more frequently.

Since 1993, when they first competed in Davis Cup, their record in head-to-head matches is 0-19. More impressively unimpressive is the fact that they have won only one set.

"I think it's wonderful to see the extremes; for me that's the beauty of the game," said Thomas Hallberg, the director of the Davis Cup, who was in attendance. "This is the lowest level of our competition, but it's also great."

Great might be stretching it. Neither the small crowds nor the spotty shotmaking was particularly electric when eight of tennis's flyweights met for five days of competition in the Botswanan capital of Gaborone last March. Nor was Gaborone itself much to e-mail home about with its wide, sun-baked streets and city-center architecture that would blend nicely with your average American on-ramp.

"I'm not saying I was expecting elephants," said Iceland's number four player Oli Sveinsson. "But I wasn't expecting something quite so, how should I put this, plain."

In fact, Botswana has plenty of elephants and exoticism farther north in its world-renowned wetland: the Okavango Delta. What this relatively lucky nation lacks is experience with Davis Cup. Its team

Even the ball girls were impressed by the lethal left-handed serve of Togo's number one, Jean Komi Loglo.

only began competing in the event last year and Gaborone only got to host the first Group IV match in history because International Tennis Federation officials developed cold sneakers with four weeks to go and pulled the event out of Sudan, whose long-simmering civil war was showing faint signs of coming to an uncivil boil.

So who could really blame that well-meaning Botswana government minister, who shall remain nameless, for taking the lectern at the inaugural dinner and referring to the grand old competition as "The DENNIS Cup." Or that smiling Gaborone taxi driver for explaining that the players he wanted to see were "Stefanie Edberg and the black, French guy with the dreadlocks." Or that enthusiastic journalist from Gaborone's *Midweek Sun* newspaper for reporting that Botswana would be playing in Djibouti on March 19, in Madagascar on March 20 and in Iceland on March 21 before returning home for three final days of intense competition on March 22, 23 and 24.

And you thought the NBA had grueling road trips.

Yes, the learning curve was as steep as an elephant's trunk in Gaborone, and in the end that was what made it worth the very long journey. Among the things I didn't spot and didn't miss at the Botswana National Tennis Centre were the following: 1) prematurely world-weary expressions on young adults with high rankings; 2) portable phones; 3) entourages; 4) security guards; 5a,b,c and d) clothing reps, sports psychologists, personal trainers and, if I may be permitted to pile on, AGENTS.

"I have never seen the people from IMG," Kasule said.

After seeing much of the play on display in Gaborone, it is difficult to fault the agents. Not one of the thirty-two men and boys who competed had an ATP point to their little-known name. With a handful of exceptions, big shots were as rare as big shots. There were slice forehands, middling footwork and unforced errors in abundance, but that does not mean it was painful to watch.

This was tennis with few strings attached. They played without prize money and without free racquets and their accompanying stencil marks shimmering brazenly in the autumn heat. About the closest the participants came to a logo was the Loglo brothers from Togo.

"They are really virgins all of them," said a slightly wistful Hallberg, speaking—I hasten to add—in a marketing sense. "We give them hats to wear, and they appreciate getting their hats and they wear their hats. Getting a Pete Sampras to wear a Davis Cup hat is not an easy thing. It happens sometimes, but here they appreciate everything. They don't really have contracts, at least not yet."

By the time the tennis stopped in Gaborone, only two nations had earned promotion to Group Three: Togo and Madagascar. And when the two most powerful flyweights in Group Four met on the final day, Madagascar ended up finishing first in its first Davis Cup event.

"For me, it's too late for Wimbledon," said twenty-seven-year-old Harivony Adrianafetra, Madagascar's number-two player. "But at least I got one of my dreams."

Published with the permission of Tennis *magazine.*

The triumphant team from Madagascar celebrate in true global fashion. Top: Madagascar's number-one player, Rija Thierry Rajoabelina.

QUARTERFINAL
ROUND

April in Pesaro: Veni vidi Camporese

To be perfectly frank, it was the sort of embrace one normally expects from honeymooners in Italy, not tennis players in Italy.

But there it was in very public view in the small, rather somnolent coastal resort of Pesaro on April 5: Diego Nargiso lying on top of his fallen doubles partner Omar Camporese near the net and hanging on for dear *dolce vita* as both men trembled with a mixture of joy and disbelief.

Camporese had just knocked away a forehand volley on match point to give the Italians an insurmountable 3-0 lead, and what made it all so improbable and emotional was that the team they were leading was heavily favored Spain.

"Sono al settimo cielo," said Camporese, who also had upset Carlos Moya in singles in the tie's opening rubber.

If Camporese was in seventh heaven, he had plenty of company on the shores of the Adriatic: there was his fellow singles player Renzo Furlan, who had upset Albert Costa. There was the Italian captain Adriano Panatta, who had cagily downplayed his team's chances and stuck by Camporese despite a world ranking that would have made most captains sniff and look for other solutions.

There were also the eight thousand rambunctious Italian fans who crowded into the Palasport Bpa arena in Pesaro each day, gleefully egging on their unlikely journeymen heroes to the most surprising victory of the 1997 Davis Cup tournament. When Camporese and Nargiso had put the final flourish on their 5-7, 7-6 (7-0), 6-2, 7-6 (7-5) victory over Francisco Roig and Javier Sanchez, the tennis *tifosi* very nearly overran the quick GreenSet Trophy surface in an attempt to share in the embrace. Luckily for Camporese's health, the attempt failed, but that didn't turn down the volume of the victory celebration.

"We were happy, unbelievably happy," Camporese said.

The Italian headline writers were in a similar frame of mind. "Miracolo Italia" wrote *Tempo* to lead off its coverage the next morning. "Il miracolo e completo" wrote *Corriere Dello Sport*.

In reality, it was more upset than miracle. Yes, Spanish singles players Moya and Costa were ranked 8th and 12th in the world respectfully. Yes, their Italian counterparts, Furlan and Camporese, were ranked 64th and 156th. But what those glaringly disparate numbers did not indicate was the gap in Davis Cup experience. While the twenty-six-year-old Furlan and twenty-eight-year-old Camporese had played for their nation on numerous occasions, the twenty-year-old Moya and twenty-one-year-old Costa had only begun competing in the event in 1996 and had yet to find themselves in the sort of knee-weakening situation that Davis Cup specializes in creating.

"Davis Cup is another sport," said Panatta, whose decision to host the tie indoors on a fast surface was another equalizer. It was an obvious choice because at the time of the quarterfinal, there was only one indoor court in Barcelona, the claycourt-covered city that the bumper crop of contemporary Spanish players use as a training base.

Though Moya, long hair flapping and huge forehand working, had beaten none other than Boris Becker on a medium-speed indoor Taraflex carpet in Paris six months earlier, he is unquestionably more

Joy reigned in Pesaro as the Italians upset Spain, the favorites, in the quarterfinals. Preceding pages: Davis Cup inspires very colorful visions of national pride.

Forza! The Italian team upset the heralded Spaniards. It was a Bacchanalian romp.

The recline and fall of the Roman empire: Omar Camporese and Diego Nargiso win the decisive point for Italy.

at ease on a high-bouncing surface like clay or Rebound Ace: the hardcourt upon which he reached the final of the Australian Open in January. In Panatta's mind, Costa was even more vulnerable indoors. And thus, while the Italian captain was busy moaning publicly that Italy had a meager "20 percent chance" of winning, he was more sanguine in private.

"I thought it was more or less 40 percent," Panatta said. "I know some kinds of players, when they play in difficult conditions, react differently. When we beat Russia in the first round in 1996, we played outdoors in Rome. It was very, very cold, and I knew that Yevgeny Kafelnikov was a little bit mad because the conditions were very, very bad. So I think I know what some kind of players think about when they play Davis Cup because I played so many matches myself."

A veteran doubles team might have proved an effective stabilizing force for the Spaniards. Instead, captain Manuel Santana curiously selected Roig, a Davis Cup rookie, and Sanchez, who had never played doubles in Davis Cup. What made the choice even more suspect was that Roig and Sanchez had never played doubles together.

"We never expected Roig would be in their team," Camporese said. "We figured Sergi Bruguera or Alex Corretja. It was good for us but a bad choice for Manolo Santana, especially on fast courts."

Five days earlier, Bruguera had reached the singles final at the prestigious Lipton Championships on hardcourts in Key Biscayne, Florida. Corretja was about to go on a springtime run on clay that would lift him into the top five. But Santana had already announced his team in March, and there would be no final-hour adjustments.

The result was another poignant addition to the Spaniards' litany of Davis Cup disappointments. When the tie began, the Spaniards had five players in the top twenty: more than any other nation, including the United States. But their relative inexperience on indoor surfaces coupled with what one Barcelona psychologist termed a "national inferiority complex" was enough to make the rankings irrelevant.

"It's a nearly anthropological phenomenon," sports psychologist Imma Puig told the French newspaper *L'Equipe*. "When the Spanish people compare themselve to other people, they consider themselves inferior. Not only in sport but in everything and though it may be changing today, it remains true. It's one of the reasons the Spaniards don't do better in team sports in general."

The ebullient Italians do not seem to suffer from the same complex. France is the only team to overachieve more in recent years in Davis Cup, but at least the French have a player like Cedric Pioline, talented enough to have reached the U.S. Open and Wimbledon singles finals. Italy hasn't had a player in a Grand Slam final since Panatta won the French Open in 1976, and with its most promising team member, Andrea Gaudenzi, suffering through an injury-plagued season, they did not have anyone in the top fifty to call on this year.

"In Italy, there is unbelievable pressure," said former player Paolo Bertolucci, who replaced Panatta as captain in September after Panatta resigned because of differences with the Italian Tennis Federation. "When you win a match at age fourteen or sixteen, you already have a contract and a manager. The crowd, the media, everybody loses their head. The players think they have arrived, and they don't know that they haven't even started yet."

Camporese accepts the criticism but disagrees with the thesis.

"Maybe that is right, but the Americans get a lot of things when they do well, and it doesn't seem to hurt the American results," he said. "Maybe there is something wrong with the Italian Federation's approach."

Feet of clay

Spain is, without doubt, the strongest tennis nation to never have won the Cup, with Romania, Russia, India and Argentina following in its choppy wake. The closest the Spaniards have come were Final appearances in 1965 and 1967 when Santana, the former Madrid ballboy, was at the peak of his considerable powers and effervescent appeal. On both occasions, the Spaniards met the Australians on grass in Australia in the challenge round, and on both occasions they lost, 4-1, to teams that featured Roy Emerson, John Newcombe and Tony Roche (the 1965 team also included Fred Stolle).

The Spaniards might well have won in 1965 if Andres Gimeno had not turned professional. They might well have won in 1967 if a Davis Cup rookie named Manuel Orantes had been closer to his apogee. But fate would have it otherwise, and thirty years later, Spain has yet to return to the Final. They have not even reached the semifinals since 1987 and spent last year fighting their way out of Group One, which, considering the strength and esprit de corps of the current generation of Spanish players, is difficult to believe.

That approach appeared set to change but, wrong or right, Davis Cup is clearly an exception to the local rule. Along with Sweden and the Czech Republic, Italy is the only nation to have remained in the World Group every year since its inception in 1981, and after reaching the semifinals in 1996 and nearly making the final before blowing a 2-0 lead against the French, Panatta and the Italians became unlikely semifinalists again in Pesaro.

"Our players are very involved in Davis Cup; they believe in Davis Cup," Panatta said. "They are very involved with the people, especially when we play in Italy. And the people who might be dissatisfied with the players' performance in the regular tournaments come out and support us. We feel like we are doing something important, and that shows."

It is also important to have a good draw, and with home ties in the first two rounds in 1996 and 1997 and no house calls from the United States or Sweden, the Italians have been nearly as blessed as their antiquity-strewn tourist magnet of a nation.

"Yes, we were lucky," Camporese said. "But we still had to beat Spain."

Probably the only people happier than the Italian players about the victory were numerologists. The last time the Italians hosted the Spaniards was in 1992 in the northerly city of Bolzano. The Italians, with Camporese in the lineup, won by the same score, 4-1, and (here comes the eerie part) the Spanish singles players, Emilio Sanchez and Bruguera, were ranked 8th and 12th, just like Moya and Costa.

Call it foreshadowing, and yet even the numerologists might not have forecast a Camporese victory in the opening singles match, particularly when he lost the first two sets to Moya in tiebreakers. But the bearded Italian, down on his luck for the last four years, has always been at his most dangerous indoors, and in Pesaro, with his languid, deceptively detached manner, he gradually wove a strong enough web to snare the more mobile, more explosive Moya. He won the last three sets with surprising swiftness—6-1, 6-3, 6-3—and was soon exchanging hugs, kisses and encomiums with his captain.

"I knew Omar could play a very good match, but he played an extraordinary match," Panatta said.

"I owe everything to Panatta," Camporese said.

That evening, an estimated eight million of Italy's fifty-eight million inhabitants tuned in as they returned from work to watch the diminutive, dogged Furlan—"il Chang italiano"—shrug off a sore left thigh and beat Costa in five, somewhat less surprising sets.

"Maybe our guys like to have revenge when they play Davis Cup because in the ATP events, they don't play so good," Panatta said with a chuckle.

As the Spaniards headed off to get their revenge in ATP events, officials at the Spanish Tennis Federation proved that they had nothing in common with their nation's chronically impatient soccer team owners by extending Santana's contract through 2000. Perhaps more important, the federation discussed plans to construct a true indoor tennis facility in Barcelona to keep future Camporeses from wreaking future havoc.

"We need it," Corretja said. "We lost to Italy because we didn't have the indoor preparation."

Santana, who, naturally, is paid to be positive, likes his team's chances of finally living up to its ability: "I think we can win the Davis Cup in the next three years," he said.

No child's play and no child for Sweden

As the Italians were keeping their hopes alive in 1997, the South Africans and Swedes were trading indoor blows of their own in Vaxjo, birthplace of Jonas Björkman and Mats Wilander and home to

On the first day of the tie, the then world number eight Carlos Moya, top, squandered a two-set lead and lost to the unheralded Omar Camporese while Italy's number one, Renzo Furlan, bottom, also staged an upset over number twelve ranked Albert Costa to give Italy a 2-0 lead.

Magnus Larsson and Stefan Edberg. With Larsson out temporarily with a toe injury and Edberg and Wilander out permanently, only Björkman would play a role in this quarterfinal. It would prove decisive as he joined forces with regular partner Nicklas Kulti to win a five-set doubles match over David Adams and Ellis Ferreira and then rallied to beat Grant Stafford in five more sets in the definitive fifth rubber.

Perhaps Björkman should have known it would be his weekend when he beat the South Africans and his teammates in a glass-blowing contest conducted before the draw. "It's so wonderful to clinch the series in my hometown," exclaimed Björkman, whose current home is actually much farther south in tax-free Monte Carlo. "It's my best Davis Cup moment since 1994 when we won the whole Cup."

Such heroics were necessary because South Africa's more famous Ferreira, Wayne, played up to his potential in both his singles matches. Ferreira had lost five straight Davis Cup singles and doubles matches before this year. He also was in the midst of a decidedly disappointing season that would see him drop well out of the top ten. But if he had played all year as he played in Vaxjo, he might finally have done some damage in a Grand Slam event. Sporting big hair and big shots, he defeated Björkman for the sixth straight time on Friday and Thomas Enqvist in straight sets on Sunday.

Surprisingly, Swedish captain Carl-Axel Hageskog did not watch any of the matches from his customary seat on the court. He had temporarily handed over his captain's duties to his assistant and longtime pupil, Anders Jarryd, Sweden's other recently retired Davis Cup stalwart. The reason for the coaching change? Hageskog's wife was ten days overdue with their second child and the captain wanted to be ready to rush to her side at a moment's notice.

Notice never came—Hageskog's daughter Anna was born two weeks after the tie—and Hageskog watched the proceedings from the front row of the stands, consulting regularly with Jarryd.

"It was a tough tie and a tough one for Anders also, but I think it was good for him and the team to see that it doesn't stand or fall with me," said Hageskog, a member of the Davis Cup coaching staff since 1984 who took over as Sweden's captain in 1995. "In all the matches, Anders and I try to help each other out anyway. We are really a two-man team. We worked together for nine years, and though I played on a high level, I have no experience as a Davis Cup player. What makes us a good combination is that Anders has plenty."

Both members of Australia's coaching duo have plenty of Cup experience, and at the end of their team's 5-0 quarterfinal romp on grass in Adelaide over the Czech Republic, John Newcombe and Tony Roche both were sprayed with champagne by their giddy charges. All in all, champagne would prove considerably more troublesome to the Australians than did the Czechs, who arrived at Memorial Drive without four of their top five players, including Petr Korda and Daniel Vacek, and then lost Jiri Novak to a high fever before he had a chance to play singles on the opening day.

Patrick Rafter, the first-round hero, defeated Martin Damm in four sets in the opening rubber. His doubles partner, Mark Philippoussis, needed four more to dispose of Novak's last-minute replacement, David Rikl. And after Woodbridge and Woodforde, playing Davis Cup in his hometown for the first time, defeated Damm and Rikl in doubles on Saturday, a very jolly Australian team headed off to the official dinner already assured of a spot in the semifinals.

There were toasts with champagne; there was revelry, and neither Philippoussis nor Rafter got to bed until very late (or very early, depending on your perspective). But the next day, they still managed to win their dead rubbers, Philippoussis beating Damm 6-4, 6-2 and Rafter beating Rikl by the schizophrenic score of 7-6 (15-13), 0-6, 6-2.

"I was still drunk coming here this morning," Rafter said afterwards. "I started sobering up halfway through—I felt great in the third set."

Although the actual tie was played on Taraflex, South Africa's Wayne Ferreira, top, and Sweden's Thomas Enqvist, bottom, also challenged each other on glass. A magical moment, opposite, in what would prove to be an exceptional year for Jonas Björkman as he won the decisive fifth rubber over South Africa's Grant Stafford to put Sweden into the semifinals.

Those ill-advised remarks would quickly raise the hackles of the Australian Medical Association and the Australian Drug Foundation who complained that Rafter and Philippoussis, who said he was hungover during his match, had sent the wrong message to the nation's youth (not to mention the wrong message to the visiting Czechs, who surely did not appreciate the implication that they could be beaten by inebriated opponents).

Rafter later apologized, saying he regretted "giving kids the wrong impression; I don't want them to think alcohol plays any part in winning matches." Newcombe, part of a generation of Australian players that never shrank from celebrating victory with great vigor, was more perplexed than shocked.

"I still to this day don't even know why Pat said what he said; there was no point in saying it," Newcombe said. "I think the thing with Pat and Mark is that neither of them drink very much alcohol. For them to say they'd drunk too much is like for me to say that I had a reasonably middle sort of night.

"I think people went overboard on it, and I think people have to respect that sometimes Pat's just a little bit too honest in that he's too trusting. So in the future, we've put a zip on his mouth. Now we say we're going to celebrate by having a glass of warm milk, and we'll be tucked in by ten o'clock at night, and if you believe that, well then go ahead and print it."

In truth this tempest in a champagne glass was one more example of why dead rubbers remain dead weight. If 3-0 leads happened rarely, they would be only a nagging concern, but of the eight first-round matches in the World Group in 1996, five were dead on the third day. In 1997, three of the first-round matches were, as were two quarterfinals.

"It's a difficult situation, but you have that responsibility to the fans who have paid for their tickets," Roche said. "A lot of the top guys don't even play dead rubbers; our guys did."

By year's end, the ITF revised Cup rules to allow captains to freely substitute on the third day if there is already a result: a change that would at least increase the odds that those who play dead rubbers are eager to compete.

What Newcombe was most eager for in Adelaide was a chance to play the United States in the semifinals: "We want Sampras and whomever else they give us," he told the crowd. Later, he explained his reasoning: "I wanted our guys to realize that I want their names on the Cup only when they've taken out the best the world has to offer."

Agassi, the stand-in star

The best was not on display in Newport Beach, California, for the quarterfinal between the United States and Holland. Despite the fact that Sampras and Chang grew up Californians and competed in the United States the week before at the Lipton Championships, both skipped the tie. More surprisingly, so did Richard Krajicek, the Dutch number one who has often struggled in Davis Cup and had recently returned to the circuit after knee surgery.

"The knee was part of it, but I also just wanted to have a break," said Krajicek, citing—like Chang and Sampras—overprogramming.

"The Dutch got a little taste of what I deal with by getting rejected by top players sometimes," Gullikson said.

The absence of Sampras and Chang relaunched a familiar debate in the United States about the best way to revitalize Davis Cup in that country. Sampras and Andre Agassi, who played in Newport Beach, have advocated holding it every two years. Others have suggested playing it out over a two-year

No worries attracting young, female fans when Australia's Patrick Rafter and Mark Philippoussis take the court.

From colony to captain's chair

Stanley Franker's father was the caretaker of a tennis club in Paramaribo, the capital of Surinam. He was also a furniture maker, and when his young son began clamoring for a racket, he did his best to improvise, constructing a paddle with a rounded grip out of light, flexible wood. Several years later, when Franker was eleven, he accompanied his father to the club and, paddle in hand, began playing another junior. "I kicked his tail," Franker remembered with a grin. "Some of the members were watching, and they told me I should try a regular racket. I found out that tennis was a lot easier with strings."

Tennis with strings would take Franker a long way from the former Dutch colony on the steamy, northern coast of South America. From 1986 until 1997, he was the technical director of the Royal Dutch Lawn Tennis Association and captain of the Davis Cup team. When Franker arrived, only one Dutch player, Michiel Schapers, was ranked among the top hundred, and no Dutch man had won a Grand Slam singles title. At the end of 1997, four men were in the top hundred and Richard Krajicek is now part of Wimbledon history after his victory in 1996.

"We had to develop a tennis culture in the country," said Franker, who turned fifty-two in November 1997. "In any good tennis country, you need institutions and heroes. We already had institutions."
In Austria, where Franker was national coach from 1983 to 1986, he was also instrumental in the development of Thomas Muster, Horst Skoff and Alex Antonitsch. He was also instrumental in the development of Charlton Heston and Sidney Poitier, whom he coached during his brief stint as a teaching pro in Beverly Hills. Apparently, there are limits to Franker's ability because neither Heston nor Poitier ever won a Slam.

period, reducing the World Group from sixteen teams to eight or giving the previous year's finalists a first-round bye. But the ITF was not biting, seeing no reason to bow to what it perceived as the demands of a handful of recalcitrant American stars.

"I'm in favor of moving with the times but, if there is an identity problem with Davis Cup, it's only in the United States," ITF president Brian Tobin later told the *New York Times*.

There are also strong market forces at work. "Having it every two years would never pass at a general meeting," said Davis Cup director Thomas Hallberg. "Davis Cup means too much. It's the major source of income for the majority of the nations and particularly the smaller nations. To just have the World Group every other or every fourth year would ruin the whole promotion and relegation system. Davis Cup is an annual event for sure, and we currently have new, long-term sponsorship contracts that commit us contractually to that."

Krajicek was not the only Dutchman struggling to fit Davis Cup into his schedule. Captain Stanley Franker already had announced that he was stepping aside after this, his eleventh, season because he wanted to lighten his massive travel load. But Franker, who played collegiately at the nearby University of Southern California, certainly would not have minded postponing his retirement with an upset in familiar surroundings.

It didn't happen, in part because Franker's hard-charging top singles player Jan Siemerink proved incapable of holding a two-set lead and in part because the struggling Agassi proved capable of recapturing some of his customary Davis Cup zeal.

Despite his glittering 22-4 career Davis Cup record, Agassi looked like anything but a world-beater upon arrival in Newport Beach. He had not won a match since February and had lost a career-worst five consecutive matches on tour. His ranking had slumped to 29. To hear him tell it, it was the price of trying to find a happy medium.

"I dedicated myself to tennis entirely for two years, working myself to the top," he told the *Los Angeles Times*. "I found myself not satisfied with the rest of my life. I felt I never had time for much else, meaning my relationships, my charitable foundation. I definitely was in a place where I was asking myself what I wanted out of this. I knew I needed more balance."

Agassi would marry actress Brooke Shields later in April, but against the Dutch, he put his mind squarely on the game for which he has such an obvious gift. "I think Andre wanted to redeem himself after not being ready for round one," said Gullikson, who had helped coach Agassi to his Olympic gold medal in Atlanta the previous summer. "Even in the past when Andre hadn't played particularly well in tournaments, he always ended up showing up strong for Davis Cup. I think he's a big match player, and I think he enjoys the support of his teammates and he certainly feeds off the energy of the crowd really well."

The sellout crowd at Palisades Tennis Club, which included a zealous block of orange-clad, orange-wigged Dutch supporters, provided plenty of energy as Agassi took the court to play Dutch number two Sjeng Schalken. Franker had picked Schalken instead of the more experienced Paul Haarhuis, and as the slender twenty-year-old struggled with his nerves and high service toss in the stiff breeze, that looked like a tactical error. Schalken would double fault ten times in three sets, which were all close but ultimately all won by a rather shaky Agassi 7-6 (8-6), 6-4, 7-6 (7-2).

That did not stop Siemerink from coming out with all guns (and volleys) blazing in a club that was previously named for the late actor John Wayne. But the Dutchman's 6-4, 6-4 lead would prove ephemeral as Courier followed Gullikson's advice and took some pace off his floundering first serve and began putting it in play more consistently. That kept Siemerink from chipping and charging and created more of the baseline rallies that Courier relishes. He won the third set 6-1, saved a match point in the tenth game of the fourth set and then won the tiebreaker with relative ease. Courier had not come back from a two-set deficit since he turned pro in 1988, but this would be his year to stare down adversity in Davis Cup, and that unflattering statistic was soon part of his past as he closed out the match 6-3 to give the U.S. a 2-0 lead.

The Dutch students with the inflatable clogs perched on their heads went back to their budget hotels feeling deflated. But after another American doubles defeat on Saturday, when Haarhuis and Jacco Eltingh handled Palisades Tennis Club member Rick Leach and Jonathan Stark in four sets, it was left to Agassi to close out the tie on Sunday morning against Siemerink. What worried Gullikson most was that it was Sunday morning.

"Andre is not a morning person," Gullikson said.

And the fact that daylight savings time had just started meant that a match that began at 11 a.m. was, according to Agassi's biological clock, beginning at 10 a.m. Not surprisingly, Siemerink came out roaring again. After all, it was 8 p.m. in Holland. But once more he proved unable to sustain his momentum as Agassi followed the same comeback blueprint as Courier, prevailing 3-6, 3-6, 6-3, 6-3, 6-3.

"I remember sitting in the locker room, watching Andre play when he was down two sets to love and seeing that he didn't have as much confidence as he normally had," Courier said. "And then Starkie came in the locker room and we were watching and Andre starts lighting it up, and I'm just saying, 'This guy is the best ballstriker in the game. All he's got to do is strike the ball because no one times the ball like he does.' And for three sets he just hit the ball so cleanly and so well."

It probably did not make Siemerink feel any cheerier to hear that Agassi had only rallied from a two-set deficit once before. "He changed his level, and I couldn't," Siemerink said. "These guys have more ability than other players. They have both been number one."

With fifteen straight victories in Davis Cup, Agassi was still number two on his nation's all-time list: one behind Bill Tilden's record of sixteen.

"If it was safe for them to say I was done, I guess it's safe for me to say I'm back," said Agassi, referring to those who had criticized him for his precipitous slide in the rankings.

His reputation would soon be in harm's way again, however, as he skipped both the French Open and Wimbledon and struggled through the summer hard-court season before resurfacing at the U.S. Open. By year's end, he was ranked below 100 and playing in challenger events with $50,000 purses.

"I think Andre doesn't have as much self-confidence as he should for the player he is," Gullikson said. "Andre is such a great ballstriker that sometimes on the days where he's not striking the ball well, I think he kind of gets disappointed in himself and stops competing. But he just kept plugging away in Newport Beach and proved he's still a great Davis Cup warrior."

The irony is that Agassi—one of the only players in the 1990s who has proved capable of capturing the American public's imagination—has done much of his best work in an event that has often proved incapable of turning American heads.

"I just wish that the average American tennis fan understood how much it takes to play these matches," Courier said. "In 1995, we went to Moscow and won the Final on the road and brought the Cup back home. There's no celebration, no trip to the White House. It's a small tidbit in the sports section because it's NFL Sunday. I think when you give up personal goals for a team goal like this, you should get some accolades."

Fifteen! With this win, Agassi was one match from tying Tilden's record for straight cup victories.

Above left and opposite: arguably the highlight of his 1997 year was Andre Agassi's stellar performance against the Dutch in the Davis Cup quarterfinal round. He defeated Jan Siemerink, above right, coming back from a two-set deficit, to win the tie.

Omar Camporese

IT WAS THE YEAR OF EGALITARIANISM in men's tennis. For the first time in history, there were unseeded finalists in all four Grand Slam events.

Davis Cup had its unlikely protagonists, too, and none was more improbable than Omar Camporese, who promptly reemerged from obscurity to lead Italy to an upset of Spain in the quarterfinals and then promptly remerged with the shadows.

Camporese, a Bologna native named incongruously for former Juventus of Turin soccer star Omar Sivori, might not possess great mobility, a great work ethic or a great tennis mind. But he still has a dream of a forehand, and when he is properly motivated and properly prepared, he is still a very dangerous customer indoors.

"We tried to help him gain some more confidence and to make him feel like he was important for the team and for the country again, and it all turned out right," said Italy's captain Adriano Panatta.

The last time the twenty-nine-year-old Camporese had played Davis Cup was in March 1993 against Brazil. Three months later, he underwent surgery for tennis elbow and missed most of the next year. The elbow had first begun troubling him during the week of his greatest success in February 1992, when he won in Milan and his ranking climbed to a career-high 18.

"Everything might have been different if not for the pain," Camporese said. Because of the pain and his own limitations, he would spend the next five years searching in vain for the same results that had allowed him to rush out and optimistically buy a Porsche with his early winnings.

"I know the guy very well," said former Italian star Paolo Bertolucci, who coached Camporese in 1996. "The problem is a mental and physical problem because when he works and is in good shape, I think he can be a very good player. I don't think he works enough during the tournaments and during the week off."

But Panatta still felt that Camporese could be useful, and so he telephoned him and asked him to play doubles in the first-round tie against Mexico in Rome. "I was really surprised," Camporese said. "I expected the call before, like two years ago, not this year when I was not playing too good."

When Andrea Gaudenzi contracted the flu, Camporese, with his triple-digit world ranking, suddenly found himself back in Italy's singles lineup and, with two weeks of good preparation, won the opening rubber against Alejandro Hernandez to improve his career Davis Cup record to 15-8 and 10-6 in singles.

"Omar likes to have many people around him to take care of him before the match," Panatta said. "I used to believe in him all the time, and I knew if I gave him a chance to play against Mexico, which was not such a tough match on clay, maybe he could be in good shape for the next match against Spain on his best surface."

Panatta's hunch proved correct as Camporese upset Carlos Moya and then teamed with longtime partner Diego Nargiso to clinch the victory in doubles and become the flavor of the month in the homeland of gelato. "When I was walking on the street, all the people, they were stopping me and saying, 'Well done, Omar,' and 'You were a hero, Omar,'" Camporese said. "But they forgot immediately, I tell you."

"You feel another way when you are 18 in the world and when you are 140-something," Camporese said. "You can play okay in Davis Cup because you play just one match or two matches, you can fight. But in a tournament, you have to play five days in a row if you want to make some points, and when you have to play qualifying and then Goran Ivanisevic in the first round, it's tough. I thought after the win against Spain, things would be right for me. I had the feeling again, the self-confidence, but it didn't happen. I played really good players like Alex Corretja in Munich and Marcelo Rios in Rome. After a time, the confidence left."

What will linger is the memory of eight thousand Italians pulling for him in Pesaro and exploding with joy after his final forehand volley. "For a moment," Camporese said, "I was the king."

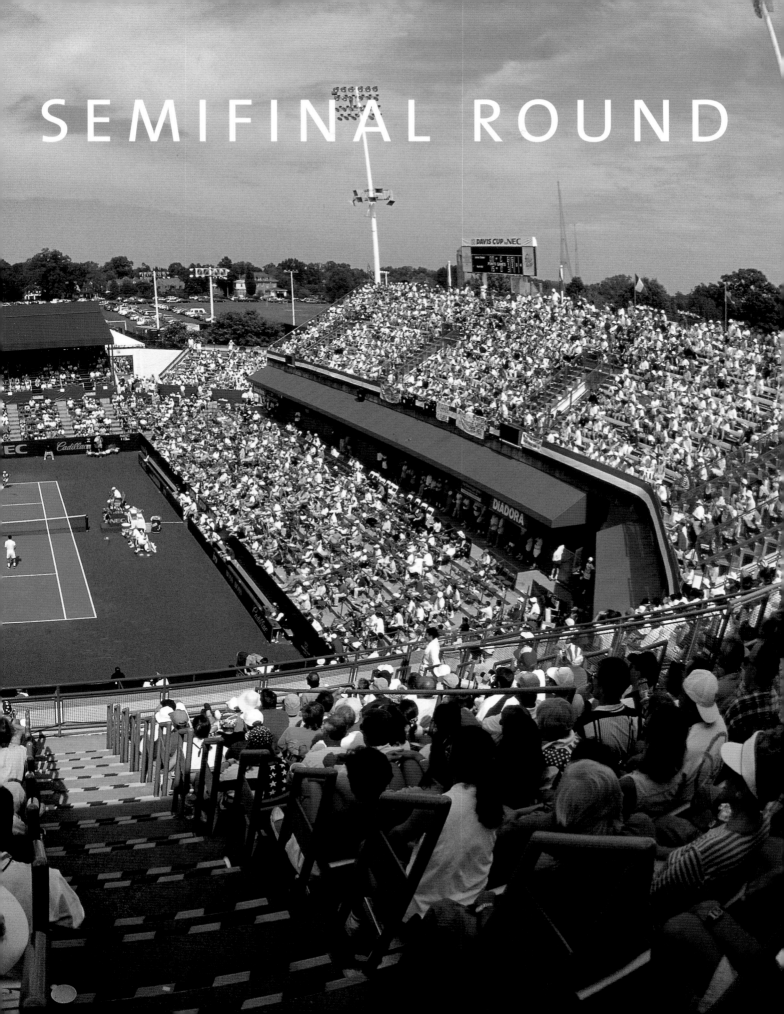

A capital adventure for the USA

THE SITE WAS THE WEST STEPS of the domed, neoclassical Capitol building in Washington D.C.: the scenic, symbolic spot where presidents are inaugurated and promises made.

Standing tall on those steps at noon on September 18 were a different sort of elite: the American and Australian Davis Cup teams, who had gathered for the draw ceremony for their semifinal. It was a warm, oppressively humid day in Washington: the kind that sends bureaucrats scurrying for something more than diplomatic cover. But there was still no predicting what was about to happen as Senator John Breaux, a voluble Democrat and tennis lover from Louisiana, marched up to the phalanx of microphones and began singing the praises of the highest-profile Aussie-American showdown in years.

Shortly after Breaux began, the United States's towering six-foot-six-inch Todd Martin teetered slightly, grabbed his captain Tom Gullikson's right shoulder and fainted. The crowd, composed largely of journalists and dignitaries, let out a collective gasp as Gullikson and Jim Courier broke Martin's lengthy fall.

For a few awkward moments, Breaux, who was standing in front of the players and had not seen Martin tumble, continued rattling on as team physicians and therapists huddled around the American. The proceedings were finally stopped and Martin, who thankfully was suffering from nothing more than the ill effects of dehydration and a stomach ailment, was soon rolled off stage and steps, dazed yet conscious, in a wheelchair.

As omens go, it was a rotten one for the Americans, but as it turned out, it was the last time they would look vulnerable in their nation's capital.

"To be honest," Gullikson said later, "we had a lot to prove to the Aussies."

As the underdog Italians arrived quietly in Norrkoping to face the heavily favored Swedes in the other semifinal, the underdog Australians arrived in Washington full of pluck and optimism in the wake of Patrick Rafter's stunning run to the U.S. Open title. It was the first singles victory by an Australian man in a Grand Slam since Pat Cash won Wimbledon in 1987 and the first at the Open since John Newcombe in 1973, and it put an entirely new spin on the showdown in a city where spin is a way of life.

Yes, the United States had the top two players in the world rankings: Pete Sampras and Michael Chang, who both finally saw fit to say "yes" to inquiring captain Gully. But Australia had Rafter, now ranked number three in the world; a loose cannon in the explosive, erratic Mark Philippoussis and the world's best doubles team in Mark Woodforde and Todd Woodbridge. It also had the sort of bonhomie and collective spirit the U.S. appeared to lack with its perpetually evolving/devolving lineup.

"Australia is so far away from anything that when they go to Europe or come to the States, they have always historically had to travel in packs to survive," Gullikson said, sparking considerable laughter at a pre-tie news conference.

But this was a case where the pack mentality would prove inferior to rugged individualism. Chang would play fine tennis against the Australians; Sampras would play superb tennis, and despite the visitor's obvious strength, the 4-1 final score was not deceptively lopsided. The Americans dominated this

One of the most impressive draw ceremonies in history, on the steps of the United States Capitol Building, was made even more dramatic when the USA's Todd Martin fainted as a result of dehydration and a stomach ailment. Preceding pages: the chance to see the three best players in the world and the number-one doubles team made a sellout a sure thing for the USA-Australia semifinal in Washington.

tie in which none of the rubbers went five sets. Their only loss came predictably in doubles against the Woodies, and it did not come easy.

"You'd expect the number one and two players in the world, when they're playing at home on a court that suits them, to play their best, and they did," Newcombe said. "These guys are not number one and two in the world for nothing, and one of the things about being good is that you have got a great competitive nature. I know from being at the top, you hate to see anyone else coming up and trying to knock you off the perch."

A whiff of the good, old, bipolar days

The United States and Australia have occupied the loftiest perch in Davis Cup more than any other nations. Entering the 1997 campaign, the United States had won the Cup a record thirty-one times; the Australians twenty-six. For one lengthy stretch—1938 to 1959—the two allies met in the Davis Cup Final, then known as the Challenge Round, every year the event was contested, and they continued to face off regularly throughout the 1960s. But such meetings have grown rarer over the years, in part because of Australia's failure to produce champions. Though the "Aussies" and "Yanks" have played each other more often than any other teams—the U.S. now leads the series 25-19—this semifinal was only their third meeting in the last decade.

"I think that's why a lot of us were really psyched up for this particular tie, because it had the makings of the ties from many, many years ago with the world's top three singles players and the world's top doubles team," Woodforde said.

It was the first time since the computer-ranking systems began that one tie had brought together so many low numbers, but in the end, the Plexipave hardcourt surface at the William H.G. FitzGerald Tennis Center would suit the Americans better. Two weeks earlier during the U.S. Open, Gullikson had sat inside the cavernous confines of the new, twenty-three-thousand-seat Arthur Ashe Stadium and concluded that the center court was playing too fast for Chang when he lost to Rafter in the semifinals.

"We resurfaced the courts right before the tie in Washington, and we got them medium slow," Gullikson said. "Our whole goal was to make it a little tougher for Rafter to serve and volley on his second serve and to make Philippoussis's serve maybe a little bit easier to return. I think we did that quite well."

Until the summer of 1997, the counter-punching Chang had handled the attacking Rafter with relative ease, winning five of their six encounters. But then in Long Island, on the eve of the U.S. Open, Rafter beat him in straight sets in the quarterfinals.

If that was unsettling to the American, what happened at the Open was devastating. With Sampras already out of the way, after being upset in the fourth round by the maddeningly uneven Petr Korda, Chang suddenly found himself the heavy favorite to win his national title for the first time. Considering that Rafter had won exactly one tournament in his career coming into the Open, it was not unreasonable to expect Chang's big-match experience would make the difference. It did not—something Chang may reflect on and regret for years to come in the same way Stefan Edberg now rues his loss to Chang in the 1989 French Open final.

During the course of Rafter's 6-3, 6-3, 6-4 victory in Queens, Chang, who has some of the best returns and passing shots in tennis, never broke him. And long after the upset had ended and the massive crowd had filed out, Carl, Chang's older brother and coach, was still sitting alone in the players' box,

Three Fs spell nostalgia

"I think the biggest thrill for all of us old Australian and American guys is that it's good to see the old rivalry again because it's fierce, fair and friendly," said Fred Stolle, the former Australian star who now works for American television. "That's what we grew up with and to be this ancient and call the matches, I still get goose bumps. Still." In 1951, when Stolle was considerably less ancient, he was a ballboy in White City in Sydney when Frank Sedgman and Ken McGregor combined to defeat the American team led by Vic Seixas and Ted Schroeder, 3-2.

"I was a pipsqueak; too small to run around much," Stolle said. "So my job was to polish the Cup. I did it every day for a week. Thank goodness it only had one level then. Now, it has two, and it will soon have three. At least now I've got my name on it a couple of times."

Australia marches on Washington: Mark Philippoussis and Patrick Rafter on Capitol Hill.

Patrick Rafter of Australia, top, Pete Sampras of the United States, middle, and Mark Philippoussis of Australia, bottom. Michael Chang, opposite, of the United States avenged his semifinal loss to Patrick Rafter at the U.S. Open by defeating him in the opening singles.

looking like someone Rodin might have sculpted as he pondered the missed opportunity.

There was more mulling prior to the opening rubber in Washington: a Chang-Rafter rematch. Two days before it, Michael's father Joe walked up to Gullikson holding a videocassette of the Open semifinal and asked if he wanted to screen it with Michael and Carl. Gullikson obliged, and he was convinced as he watched that there was no reason for Chang to remake himself. He had beaten Rafter five out of six times before August. It was simply a question of executing his already sound gameplan and letting the slower court take effect.

And so, though Chang joked before the match about "serving and volleying" himself, each player remained very much in character on Friday, and this time, Carl did not have to linger in the stands after the cheering stopped. Chang won 6-4, 1-6, 6-3, 6-4. He broke Rafter six times in all, but the key point came on his own serve with Rafter leading 3-1, 30-40 in the third set. The athletic Australian was getting his big, soft hands around the match at that stage, but Chang came up with an ace wide in the ad-court to save the break point. He would go on to win nine of the next ten games, screaming with delight as he walked toward Gullikson after breaking Rafter with one of his trademark topspin forehand lobs to take a 4-1, two-break lead in the final set.

Clearly, Rafter was not as sharp as he had been at the Open: he would miss too many forehand volleys on top of the net and double fault nine times overall. But he showed his newfound maturity and self-confidence by refusing to fold, breaking Chang in the next game and cagily staying back more often to break the American's rhythm.

"Come on Rafter!" yelled a female high in the stands. Considering Rafter's rugged good looks, such support was hardly shocking. What was surprising was that the female voice was an American voice. But Chang, even without an absolute homecourt advantage, held firm and was soon serving for the rubber at 5-4.

On his second match point at 40-30, he hit a forehand passing shot. As soon as it crossed the net, the opening strains of a John Philip Sousa tune blasted out of speakers within the stadium. But someone had jumped the gun. Rafter hit a backhand volley into the open court and chair umpire Jorge Dias called a let. Rafter would save two more match points and squander a break-point opportunity of his own before Chang finally gave the United States a 1-0 lead with his eleventh ace followed by a service winner. It was an appropriate finish, considering Chang had served extremely well under pressure all match, and this time, no one had to stop the music.

"In a sense, the U.S. Open loss will always be disappointing," Chang said after exchanging high fives with his teammates. "It would be nice to be able to have won both, but then again, sometimes things don't go the way you want them to."

Things certainly did not go Mark Philippoussis's way during the next match. He watched, often quite helplessly, as Sampras swept to a 6-1, 6-2, 7-6 (7-5) victory that Gullikson quite aptly termed "a clinic." The two power players' most famous previous encounter was in the third round of the 1996 Australian Open when Philippoussis served brilliantly to defeat Sampras in straight sets and sent his nation into a very ephemeral frenzy (he lost convincingly to Woodforde in the next round). But this was Sampras's third straight victory over the erratic Philippoussis in important settings, and for much of the first two sets, the nervous Scud looked about as threatening as a missile without a launcher.

"My feet weren't moving," Philippoussis said.

Sampras's were, however, and when he is gliding about a court with such ease and ripping his shots with such focus and conviction, it is not at all difficult to understand why he has been the world's

The Americans on grass

The American Davis Cuppers might play tennis for a living, but they are almost as serious about playing golf for fun. And in 1997, captain Tom Gullikson organized outings for his team at two of the most celebrated courses in the United States. In May, Sampras, Courier, Martin, Richey Reneberg and Gullikson played Augusta National in Augusta, Georgia, the site of the Masters. In September, shortly before they began practicing in Washington D.C., the Americans traveled to Congressional Country Club in nearby Bethesda, Maryland, site of the 1997 U.S. Open (the Australians politely declined Gullikson's invitation).

So what is it about golf and tennis players?

"I think it's a way of relaxing and yet still competing with your friends: betting a couple of bucks and playing for a little pride and bragging rights," Gullikson said. "Obviously these guys are all in great shape, so it's not like they play golf for exercise. They play golf to maybe get away from tennis a little bit, and they all play quite well."

Perhaps, but their captain plays better—at least on Grand Slam courses. His 80 at Augusta and 78 at Congressional were both low scores.

"These guys are more worried about their tennis, and I'm more worried about their tennis and my golf," Gullikson said. "That gives me the advantage."

top player for most of this decade. He would finish with seventeen aces and two double faults and win 88 percent of the points on his first serve and 61 percent on his second: impressive figures on grass, much less on a medium-slow hardcourt.

Philippoussis is most dangerous when in good position, his large body squarely set to generate awesome power, but Sampras kept him lunging and scrambling, and with Philippoussis serving at 5-5, 30-30 in the final set, Sampras even did his best to topple a few stereotypes by atypically exhorting the sell-out crowd of seventy-five thousand to cheer after he smashed an overhead.

"Maybe I am going to show a little bit more of that over the years, but I think you will still see the same Pete Sampras," he said of his cheerleading. "There are just certain times you need to kind of raise your intensity and that was one of the times."

There would be more the very next day. After trying and failing with established doubles players in the first two rounds, Gullikson decided long before the semifinals that Sampras would be playing doubles against the Australians. The problem was choosing a partner. Initially it was to be Courier, the early-season Cup hero who had been unceremoniously but understandably bounced from the singles lineup in Washington.

"No question Jim's loyalty and commitment have been awesome this year, and throughout my tenure as captain he's been great," Gullikson explained. "But I've got to look at everything, and it's my job to put the best possible team out there. Even though I like to be loyal to guys who are loyal to me, Jim struggled mightily all summer with the exception of winning the tournament in Los Angeles. When you've got the number one and two players in the world available and playing on their best surface, it's hard to say, 'Let's put somebody else in.'"

Despite his hotly competitive nature, Courier gracefully accepted his singles demotion: "I kind of feel a little bit out of place not playing, because on the practice court, I don't really know what to do," he said. "I never come to a tournament and not play. So it's kind of strange, but I also feel like I need to be here because I'm part of this team. Whatever it takes to get the job done, I want another ring."

Ultimately, what it took for Courier to get the job done in Washington was sitting and cheering. Martin was chosen for the doubles, even though he was not one of the four players initially named to the American team. Like Courier, Martin also has been loyal to Gullikson, consistently making Davis Cup a top priority. When he returned to the tour at the U.S. Open after a six-month layoff, due largely to elbow surgery, he beat Courier in the first round and soon received an invitation to practice with the team.

By draw time, Gullikson had decided to bump Alex O'Brien from the four-man roster and insert Martin, who then proceeded to faint on the Capitol steps after having what he speculated was "a reaction to some anti-inflammatory medication." The irony was that this was not the first time Martin had collapsed in front of Gullikson. In April 1996, before a quarterfinal match in Prague against the Czechs, Martin began complaining to Gullikson of stomach pains during dinner, and once the American players returned to the hotel and began playing cards, he complained again, stumbled into the hallway and collapsed. Team physician George Fareed rushed to his side and declared that he probably had food poisoning. Meanwhile, Martin winced and grabbed at his knee and yelled about a fracture, which Fareed soon confirmed as Martin was carried into the training room.

That was when Martin yelled, "April Fool's!" and Fareed started roaring with laughter.

"The Lord works in strange ways," Gullikson said in Washington, after being assured his large charge was in fine fettle. "He gets back at guys like that who pull those practical jokes."

Unfortunately for Gullikson, the less ethereal Woodies also got the best of Martin on Saturday, defeating him and Sampras, 3-6, 7-6 (7-5), 6-2, 6-4. It was a vital point for Australia and a symbolic point for all those who value doubles in this age of compulsive overemphasis on singles. The Woodies, with their nine Grand Slam doubles titles and relatively low profiles, were well aware of that symbolism, even more so after their surprising first-round loss at the U.S. Open and subsequent and uncharacteristic sniping in the press.

"I think that's why you saw Todd and I hugging each other a lot more than usual at the end," said Woodforde, who played a remarkably steady match and kept his team afloat while the more combustible Woodbridge fought to shed an acute case of tightness early.

Woodforde saved a set point at 4-5 in the second set with a wide ace. Then in the ensuing tie-breaker, when a controversial call gave the Americans a 2-0 lead, Woodbridge walked up to Dias and shrieked, "What are you doing!?"

"I was ready for Todd's tonsils to pop out," Woodforde said.

Gullikson was ready for Woodbridge to get a warning. Neither happened, but the primal scream therapy proved liberating to Woodbridge, who was a sharper, better player the rest of the way.

"It woke him up," Gullikson admitted. "In my mind, if we win that second set, we win the match."

Rome smolders while America slumbers

By the time the Americans and Australians returned to the courts on Sunday, the Swedes, six time zones away in their coastal city of Norrkoping, already had clinched their second straight spot in a Davis Cup final. The Swede who clinched it was the same Swede who had won the decisive rubber against the South Africans in the quarterfinals: Jonas Björkman.

Björkman's 4-6, 6-4, 6-0, 6-4 victory over Renzo Furlan in the fourth rubber was no surprise to anyone who had followed the two nations' diverging tennis fortunes throughout 1997. While Björkman could exult in his run to the semifinals of the U.S. Open, the best Italian performance in a Grand Slam event in 1997 was Furlan's considerably shorter run to the third round at the Australian Open. On the eve of this tie, Furlan—the highest-ranking Italian—was just 84th. Omar Camporese, the team's other singles player, had slipped to 220.

Davis Cup, of course, has made a habit of making mischief with rankings and statistics (see France vs. USA in the 1991 Final in Lyon) and the Italians had made plenty of mischief themselves against the Spaniards in the quarterfinals. The Italians no longer had the support of thousands of unabashedly subjective fans and they had experienced major off-court distractions leading up to the semifinal. Adriano Panatta, the captain since 1984 who had helped engineer the quarterfinal upset of Spain, had resigned in July after the latest in a series of increasingly public disputes with the Italian Tennis Federation president Paolo Galgani, who rejected a plan submitted in part by Panatta, proposing methods to put Italian tennis back on track.

"I don't want to be involved with politics anymore," Panatta said. "It was a very hard decision."

With Panatta in early retirement, the search for a new captain was on, and after at least one Italian tennis icon (Nicola Pietrangeli) declined the honor, Paolo Bertolucci agreed to accept what his friend and former doubles partner Panatta had relinquished—a decision Panatta reportedly interpreted as a mild form of betrayal. As if this soap opera needed any more suds, there was also a threatened lawsuit from Furlan's coach Riccardo Piatti, who was angered by some of Panatta's public remarks.

Omar Camporese of Italy, top. New Italian captain Paolo Bertolucci, bottom, stepped into the shoes of Adriano Panatta.

Renzo Furlan, top, won Italy's only point upsetting Thomas Enqvist, bottom, in five sets in the second singles. Preceding pages: the cheers were all for Sweden as the Italian doubles pair of Diego Nargiso and Omar Camporese, bottom left, overwhelming in the quarterfinals against Spain, were overwhelmed themselves in the semifinals by the exquisite teamwork of Jonas Björkman and Nicklas Kulti, top right. Although he sat on the sidelines for the semifinals, Magnus Larsson, shown lifting Swedish captain Carl-Axel Hageskog, was an integral part of the celebrations when Sweden defeated Italy to earn a place in the Final.

There were also reports of a legal tussle—between Bertolucci and his former pupil Camporese from whom he split in 1996—but that thankfully proved fictitious. "I would not have become captain if there was a lawsuit pending," said Bertolucci, who freely confessed that "when it comes to politics, we Italians are a little crazy."

Amidst all the cacophony, it was easy to forget how remarkable it was that the Italians—so mediocre individually—had managed to reach the semifinals for the second consecutive year. Even divided, they were not easy to conquer on the medium-speed Taraflex carpet the Swedes chose for a surface. On the first day, with Panatta watching on television at home, Camporese pushed Björkman to five sets, while Furlan, one of the game's tougher competitors, pushed 15th-ranked Thomas Enqvist to five sets and won, 3-6, 6-3, 6-4, 3-6, 6-3.

It was Enqvist's first official match in four weeks. He missed the U.S. Open because of a serious case of influenza and had missed the French Open and Wimbledon earlier in the year because of a freak foot injury. But it was still a fine victory for Furlan—one he called the best of his Davis Cup career.

"I beat Costa in the quarterfinals, but it's a bit different to win on the road and especially in Sweden," he said.

Asked after the first day if Italy's chances of victory were now 50 percent, the irrepressible Bertolucci quickly answered, "Oh, no."

He was right. There would not be another Italian renaissance in Europe. On Saturday, Björkman and his regular partner Nicklas Kulti, fresh off their run to the U.S. Open final, sauntered into the Norrkoping arena with the comically lengthy name—at least to an English speaker—of Himmelstalundshallen and made remarkably quick work of Camporese and Diego Nargiso. They won 6-1, 6-1, 6-2 in one hour and forty-five minutes, and Edberg, quickly becoming a regular guest of honor at Sweden's ties, said he could not "recall seeing a better doubles match with Swedes involved." That was high praise indeed considering that Edberg has both watched and played with Anders Jarryd and Mats Wilander.

"It was a nightmare," Nargiso said. "I cannot remember having lost a match where I felt so totally powerless."

All that remained was for Björkman to win his third live rubber in three days, which he soon did in style against Furlan, thereby proving that there are limits to Davis Cup's inherent wackiness.

"Seven and a half hours of hard work," said Swedish captain Carl-Axel Hageskog, summing up Björkman's time sheet. "It was a brilliant performance."

And a relatively routine performance for the Swedish team, which was now in its eleventh final since 1975. With a six-hour time difference between Norrkoping and Washington D.C., the Swedes' opponent had yet to be determined. The Australians optimistically had made a formal request of the Swedes before the semifinals even began to hold the Final after Christmas in Australia if both their teams won.

The Swedes had agreed to consider that proposal, but by the time Sampras had finished with Rafter, it was clear that the only foreigners making formal requests of the Swedes should have been Americans.

The Open champ and the all-time great

With the third consecutive sellout crowd in place on the coolest day of the tie, Rafter won the first set in a gem of a tiebreaker. The key point in that breaker came when he was trailing 5-3 on Sampras's serve with Sampras in good position at the net. Rafter hit a backhand passing shot—not his strength—

which struck the tape, flew past the surprised Sampras and landed in the corner for a winner.

But when Rafter walked to his chair up one set to love after fifty-four often exhilarating minutes, Newcombe knew better than to let him celebrate.

"I told him to take some deep breaths because, 'This bloke is going to come at you with everything he's got the next couple games,'" Newcombe said. "That's just what Pete did."

In less than fifty minutes, Sampras was the one leading by a set after ripping through Rafter 6-1, 6-1. "I can't play any better," Sampras said. "I did everything that I could do very well."

"Those were probably two of the most flawless sets of tennis I've witnessed, and I've seen a lot of tennis," Gullikson said.

And even though the final set was not quite so flawless, Sampras was still on a higher plane. A look at the statistics after he closed out the match 6-4 was enough to give a tennis junkie goose bumps. In four sets, Rafter never had a break point. Sampras served fourteen aces and one double fault. He made sixty-two winners and only fifteen unforced errors (none in the tide-turning second set). He won 85 percent of the points off his first serve and 68 percent off his second. In all, he won one hundred and thirty points to Rafter's ninety.

"I think I am at the point in my career where I don't need to prove anything," Sampras said. "But sure, when Pat won the Open, he knew coming into this weekend that he was a bit of a marked man. And when someone wins a Slam, you want a piece of that."

For Rafter, so rattled by the breeze and Sampras's brilliance that he appeared temporarily to have forgotten how to toss the ball up to serve, it was a stark reminder of the gap still separating him from the top.

"I've got a lot to learn, a lot to do before I can consolidate myself where I am now," he said. "It makes me want to work harder. That's all that it does."

Rafter could have been speaking for his teammates, because the Australians, soundly and fairly beaten though they were, have every intention of recreating a genuine rivalry.

"We'll have the war drums beating down in Australia and the noise will go right across the Pacific," Newcombe said. "We want them at our national tennis center with fifteen thousand Aussies barracking for us. It'll be twelve months down the line. We're going to be better. They're not going to get any better, and I think we can eke it out, 3-2."

Until then, the Australians will have a hard time forgetting the sound of seven thousand, two hundred American fans roaring as Sampras took a victory lap in Washington, the American flag draped around his shoulders looking suspiciously like Superman's cape. Chang and Gullikson would take the next two laps, but the fans wanted more: "We want Jim! We want Courier! We want Jim! We want Courier!"

Reluctantly, awkwardly, Courier—no sweat on his brow—walked onto the court with the flag bunched up in his hand like a star-spangled warmup suit and waved it at the crowd. Davis Cup might no longer inspire the same zeal in the United States as it does in faraway Australia, but at least the tennis fans have retained their sense of justice. If Courier had not been willing to do the dirty work earlier in the year, Sampras would never have had the chance to play the hero and some of the best tennis of his life.

Strong words from Australia's strongman

"I think our match with the United States in September gave the Davis Cup a shot in the arm in that country. Now it needs a couple more shots. It needs a bit more of a vocal commitment from the players as to what Davis Cup means to them. It's not really good enough to play one Davis Cup match a year and run around waving the flag. You need to be committed to the common cause. The American players need to verbally commit, and they need to get together with one another and decide how they are going to treat Davis Cup for the year. They have so many great players that they could field different teams in the early rounds, but they need to make it clear that they are all together. If they did that, the public would accept it. But the players need to realize that you can't just treat something lightly that has been around for a hundred years. Every two years is hogwash. That's people saying, 'We need the Davis Cup to fit with our busy schedule of making appearances and making money.' If you are going to treat the Davis Cup like that, well let's just scrap the Davis Cup. Let's treat it for what it is: the history of the game."
John Newcombe

USA! USA! For the first time the world's top three players were in one tie. Two were Americans.

Flags flew and victory laps were in order as the United States reached its fifty-ninth Davis Cup Final: world number two Michael Chang, opposite left; Captain Tom Gullikson, opposite right; Jim Courier, who anchored the team in the opening rounds against Brazil and the Netherlands, above left, and the best player of his generation and arguably of all time, world number one Pete Sampras, above right.

Pete Sampras

IT HAD BEEN NEARLY TWO YEARS since Pete Sampras served for his country; nearly two years since he came as close to winning a Davis Cup on his own as this venerable competition allows.

Sampras was responsible for two singles rubbers and the doubles in that 1995 Final against the Russians, shrugging off severe cramps, a slow claycourt surface and the throaty cheers of 18,000 neo-capitalistic *glitteratski* in Moscow to give his nation a 3-2 victory.

It was one of the shining moments in a career that has hardly lacked for points of light, but instead of transforming Sampras into a diehard Davis Cupper, his draining, dramatic performance actually encouraged him to keep his distance. In Sampras's mind, the physical and psychological price had been too high, and the reward too low, or at least too intangible.

"I didn't really know what to expect afterward," Sampras said. "I just know it was one of the best efforts I've ever put into tennis as far as what I did there. I don't want to say it went unnoticed, but Americans are supposed to win everything. And when I got home, I had a little time off, and I started getting ready for Australia, and that was pretty much it."

Said Tom Gullikson: "I was shocked at the lack of excitement when we got back. It was like it didn't even happen, like people were thinking 'We're used to our players playing like that, dragging themselves off the clay and winning three matches.'"

And so Sampras focused on more personal goals in 1996 and the first half of 1997, entertaining Gullikson's pleas and politely declining. "I usually ask him right after I pay the bill for dinner," Gullikson cracked. "But he's had a pretty good year. I think he could probably afford to take me out for a couple of dinners."

At least Sampras put his Davis Cup sabbatical to good use. During the quarterfinals, while his once and future teammates were busy with the Netherlands on the California coast, Sampras was farther inland taking the first nature hike of his life with soon-to-be girlfriend Kimberly Williams. "It was an athletic first date, to see if she can keep up with me," Sampras told the *Washington Post*.

Athletics have long come easy to Sampras, a prodigy who won the first of his ten Grand Slam singles titles at age nineteen, but Davis Cup has been a slower learning process. His first tie was the 1991 Final against the French in Lyon, and he lost both his singles rubbers to Henri Leconte and Guy Forget, who had been tuned to a perfect emotional pitch by their captain and friend Yannick Noah.

"I was so overwhelmed with Davis Cup when I first got into it," Sampras said. "That Final in Lyon, you couldn't ask for a tougher situation, and I froze." It took time for him to thaw. He would emerge victorious in only five of his first ten Cup singles matches: not the sort of winning percentage to which he or his fans have grown accustomed. But in Moscow and Washington, the two capitals that were once so diametrically and ideologically opposed, Sampras made it clear that he has learned how to handle, if not necessarily relish, the special pressures of team competition. Perhaps it helped in Washington that he had something personal to prove after his fourth-round loss in the U.S. Open. He responded with his seventh and eighth consecutive victories in Cup play.

"Pete had that look in his eye all weekend," Gullikson said. "The sort of look you really don't want to see if you're facing him across the net."

Rafter, one of those who had to face him, said "I've never seen Pete that pumped up inside."

Newcombe, one of those who had to scramble for solutions, said, "He can't play any better. That was his absolute peak. I thought having only played three tournaments since Wimbledon and having lost in the U.S. Open, he might be struggling to find his best form. But Jesus, he played unbelievably."

There was indeed a whiff of the otherworldly to Sampras's Aussie-thumping, fist-pumping performance in Washington, the city where he was born in 1971. There was a whiff of finality, as well, which may explain, in part, the reaction of some fans who approached him and congratulated him for winning the Cup. Clearly, the fans were not Swedish.

WORLD GROUP
QUALIFYING
ROUND

THE TEAMS

AUSTRIA
ZIMBABWE
NEW ZEALAND
BRAZIL
CHILE
INDIA
BELGIUM
FRANCE
GERMANY
MEXICO
ROMANIA
RUSSIA
SLOVAK REPUBLIC
CANADA
KOREA
SWITZERLAND

Always a dangerous opponent, Thomas Muster, above, won both of his singles matches in Austria's 3-2 loss to Zimbabwe and also demonstrated his prowess on the soccer field in Harare. Wayne Black, opposite, who defeated Gerald Mandl in the fifth and decisive rubber to give Zimbabwe its win over Austria, called this the "best day of my life." Preceding pages: Belgium's fortresses would become symbolic of their nation's play against France

Black days in Harare for Austria

IT WAS 5-0 IN THE LAST SET of the last rubber in Harare, and Wayne Black, racquet and match in hand, looked in the stands at his older brother, Byron, and the other members of Zimbabwe's Davis Cup team and asked just the slightest bit prematurely: "So what are we doing after this?"

Moments later, Wayne finished off Gerald Mandl and Austria and thrust his arms into the air. He was about to find out what they were doing.

"I see my brother coming at me like a full-running train with absolutely no intention of slowing down," Wayne said. "We both go crashing to the floor, and then ten guys come piling on top of us and then twenty guys pick me up and carry me on their shoulders for a couple of minutes. Unbelievable. Best day of my life."

Globalization has become more than a global buzzword at the end of the twentieth century, and the Davis Cup did not escape the trend in 1997. Tennis is not gathering momentum in all of the world's nations, but with talent, expertise and information flowing with increasing ease across once-tight borders, the game has clearly expanded its reach if not its grasp.

How else to explain the deliciously far-flung nature of the World Group Qualifying Round, which was held on the same three days in mid-September as the World Group semifinals?

The eight ties were staged on five different continents: Africa, North America, South America, Asia and Europe. And when the last serve had been smacked and the last banner brandished, teams from four different continents had earned promotion. Two of those teams—Zimbabwe and the recently independent Slovak Republic—had never reached the World Group.

The Zimbabweans, or as they are called, the Black brothers, were the bigger surprise as they upset former world number one Thomas Muster and the Austrians, 3-2, on an indoor hardcourt in the Zimbabwean capital. The Blacks had wanted to play on grass: an understandable request considering that they had learned the game from their father, Don, on four grasscourts at the family farm near Harare. But to the Blacks's chagrin, the Zimbabwe Tennis Federation was unable to come up with a site that met competitive requirements, so they had to face the Austrians on a surface that was ominously similar to the one on which Muster won the prestigious Lipton Championships in Florida six months earlier.

"We should have had the matches at our house," Wayne joked. "But my mom wouldn't have been able to cook for all those people."

Even with approximately five thousand Zimbabweans cheering against him, Muster would win both his singles matches, demolishing Wayne on Friday in straight sets after Byron had done the same to Gilbert Schaller, and then outlasting Byron in the fourth rubber on Sunday 3-6, 6-3, 2-6, 6-3, 6-1. But the Blacks would win the rubbers that mattered most, although if Muster had deigned (or dared?) to play doubles, that match might have been a great deal more suspenseful than the Blacks's straight-set victory over Georg Blumauer and the unfortunate Mandl, in which the brothers lost only thirteen points in fifteen service games.

Top to bottom: Dominik Hrbaty of Slovak Republic; Grant Connell of Canada; Karol Kucera of Slovak Republic and Daniel Nestor of Canada.

In the second set of that match, someone handed a young boy a huge Zimbabwean flag and sent him on court, where he did a premature victory lap as the crowd roared. When the tie ended on Sunday with Wayne's 5-7, 6-3, 6-3, 6-0 victory, the Zimbabwean jogging a lap with the flag was Don Black, who had played at Wimbledon as a young man when Zimbabwe was white-ruled and called Rhodesia. His only sons had come close to putting Zimbabwe in the World Group in 1995, losing 4-1 to Petr Korda and the Czechs on clay in Prague in the Qualifying Round. But this year, they got a huge break in the second round of Group One play in London when Britain's top two singles players Greg Rusedski and Tim Henman were forced to sit out the tie with injuries. The Blacks won, 4-1, at Crystal Palace and then beat a full-strength Austrian team to make Zimbabwe the second African nation in history to qualify for the World Group and write an emotional end to a remarkable year for the family (younger sister Cara won Grand Slam junior titles at Wimbledon and the U.S. Open).

Zimbabwe, a relatively underdeveloped nation with a population of eleven million, might be low in the world rankings in life expectancy, literacy and per capita GDP, but in at least one category, it was now in the top 16.

"I'm so happy to put it on the map somehow," Wayne said. "That's one of my goals for my career."

Divide and conquer

The Blacks were not the only ones dabbling in cartography. The Slovakians were doing the same as they disposed of the Canadians, 4-1, on a fast Supreme Court carpet in Montreal to complete a rapid rise from the depths of Davis Cup to its sunlit uplands.

Slovakia was created at the stroke of midnight on January 1, 1993, when Czechoslovakia's two halves peacefully went their separate ways after a disagreement over power sharing. Though independence appeared to break up one of the world's most successful tennis nations, the Czech half was always the strongest, producing players like Jan Kodes, Martina Navratilova, Ivan Lendl, Hana Mandlikova and, most recently, Jana Novotna and Petr Korda.

Of all the former stars, only Miloslav Mecir could be considered Slovakian. After winning the 1988 Olympic gold medal, reaching the finals of the U.S. Open and Australian Open and earning the sobriquet "Big Cat," Mecir's career ended prematurely because of a chronic back injury. But tennis has remained his profession, and when Slovakia arrived full of optimism in Montreal, the captain was Mecir.

Like many former Czechoslovakians, Mecir is part of a family tree with variegated branches. He is the son of a Slovakian mother and Czech father. And though he lives in the Slovakian capital of Bratislava, his wife is a Czech.

"For me, the border is something I don't like," he once said. "Until three months before the split, I still couldn't believe it could happen. But at the end, nothing could stop it, even though I don't think most of the people wanted it in their heart."

While the Czechs continued merrily on in the World Group, the Slovakians had to start over. They fielded their first team in 1994, and with two young players, Karol Kucera and Jan Kroslak, did not drop a set in earning promotion out of Group III, which was then the competition's lowest level. The following year, they lost to Egypt on clay in Cairo, but that would be their only setback, as they qualifed for Group One in 1996 and then defeated Israel and Canada in 1997 to join the Czechs among the elite.

"It's something I didn't expect with the rankings our players had when we started four years ago," Mecir said.

Though Slovakia has suffered from a shortage of tennis facilities and a lack of organizational expertise, its players have progressed rapidly, and unlike Ludmila Richterova, a talented young Slovakian woman who opted for Czech nationality, the best men have stayed faithful to their new flag.

By 1997, the twenty-three-year-old Kucera, now coached by Mecir, was considered one of the most dangerous floaters in any Grand Slam singles draw. In July, he reached the finals in Stuttgart on clay and would later win in the Czech city of Ostrava on carpet in October. He came to Canada with a 15-1 record in Davis Cup singles and left, despite the ill effects of the flu, with a 17-1 record. The other Slovak singles player was nineteen-year-old Dominik Hrbaty, the baseliner who had come within a few points of becoming an overnight sensation in the fourth round of the 1997 Australian Open, where he led world number one Pete Sampras 4-2, 15-40 on Sampras's serve in the fifth set.

Together, Kucera and Hrbaty would prove too polished for Canadians Sebastien Lareau and Daniel Nestor, who had struggled through a forgettable 1997 season and were ranked 126 and 185. Even Lareau's decision to fly all the way to Hawaii shortly before the tie to receive instruction on his serve from coach Peter Burwash proved ineffectual (not that flying to Hawaii should be construed as suffering).

About the only good news for the Canadians was provided by longtime Davis Cup stalwart and former world number-one doubles player Grant Connell, who teamed with Nestor to defeat Hrbaty and Kroslak in straight sets to cut the Slovakian lead to 2-1. But even that victory was tinged with melancholy in that it was the final match of Connell's twelve-year professional career.

"I liked the rocking chair but I hated the slippers," said the thirty-one-year-old Connell, referring to his retirement gifts from his teammates.

The only gift Kucera wanted after defeating Lareau 5-7, 6-2, 6-4, 6-3 to clinch victory on Sunday was a good and symbolic draw in the 1998 Davis Cup: "I want the Czechs at home," he said.

His wish would not be granted. The Slovaks were drawn to host the Swedes, but from the lean and hungry look of Kucera, Hrbaty and their bearded captain Mecir, Slovakia is a World Group rookie the Swedes and other teams rich in Davis Cup tradition had best not take lightly.

Where cows are sacred

No one should take Chile lightly either now that Marcelo Rios has emerged as one of the world's most dangerous (and cantankerous) players. But even with a player of Rios's ability, playing India at home on grass is often a thankless task. Just ask Goran Ivanisevic and the Croatians who stumbled in New Delhi in the 1995 World Group Qualifying Round.

The Chileans would stumble too, losing 3-2 in the same capital city, but there was no blaming Rios. The pony-tailed Chilean thinks that grass is better fit for cows than tennis—a view he reiterated in India—but for a recalcitrant, he can play rather well on it. After reaching the fourth round at Wimbledon, he won both his singles matches in New Delhi, defeating Mahesh Bhupathi in the second rubber on Friday and, much more impressively, Leander Paes in the fourth rubber on Sunday.

In Friday's opening rubber, Paes had handled Gabriel Silberstein, Chile's second singles player, with considerable ease, which was hardly surprising considering that the 183rd-ranked Silberstein had not played on grass all year. On Saturday, Paes and Bhupathi would have to work much harder to beat Rios and his new and very promising seventeen-year-old partner Nicolas Massu, a surprise pick by captain Patricio Cornejo. The heavily favored Indian pair, which emerged as one of the world's best teams in

Patriot games

In 1996, Leander Paes won a bronze medal in singles at the Summer Olympics to become the first Indian in forty years to win an Olympic medal in an individual event. That somehow seemed appropriate considering that Paes had been conceived in 1972 in the middle of the Summer Olympics in Munich (his father was on India's bronze-medal-winning field hockey team; his mother on its basketball team).

"I don't know what happened; they were supposed to be concentrating on sport, not mucking around," Paes said. But though his rankings have remained in triple digits for much of his career, he deserves a much lower number when he plays for his vast nation. His career record in Davis Cup before the victory over Chile was 34-20.

"Most people see Davis Cup as pressure on their shoulders," said the extroverted Paes, who was named India's "1996 Sportsperson of the Year" by its leading sports magazine.

"For me, Davis Cup puts pressure under my shoulders, pressure that lifts me up. I realized very early that I performed very well under pressure. The bigger the crowd and the bigger the situation, the better I do."

1997, would end up surviving 3-6, 6-3, 6-4, 6-7 (3-7), 6-3 in three hours and twenty-eight minutes.

If the fifth set had gone differently, Chile would probably have qualified for the World Group for the first time since 1985 because Rios defeated Paes in four sets on Sunday. But in the fifth and final rubber, Bhupathi erased a two-set lead by Silberstein to win 6-7 (4-7), 4-6, 6-4, 6-4, 6-3 to put India back in the World Group for the fourth time in the last five years.

Gaga over Guga

Russia, Germany, Switzerland and Brazil also would keep their spots. The Russians, playing at home in Moscow, would have to work the hardest. After jumping out to a 2-0 lead on Friday with Alexander Volkov's four-set defeat of Andrei Pavel and Yevgeny Kafelnikov's straight-set victory over Ion Moldovan, the Romanians staged a comeback. First Pavel and Gabriel Trifu upset Kafelnikov, one of the world's best doubles players, and partner Andrei Olhovskiy 6-4, 6-4, 6-4. Then Pavel embarrassed Kafelnikov again the next day in front of his home crowd, winning 6-4, 3-6, 6-4, 6-1 in the fourth rubber. If Adrian Voinea, Romania's second single player, had been healthy and playing well, the Russians might have been ripe for relegation. But in the decisive fifth rubber, Volkov handled Moldovan with relative ease 6-4, 6-3, 7-5.

Germany, Switzerland and Brazil needed only two days to clinch victory. The Germans, with semi-retired star and future Davis Cup team manager Boris Becker back in the lineup on his best surface, routed the Mexicans 5-0 on carpet in Essen. The Swiss, led by Marc Rosset, beat the South Koreans, 3-2, on carpet in Locarno, dropping both dead rubbers on a final day in which Rosset took a well-deserved rest from the rigors of carrying his small nation on his sloping shoulders.

The Brazilians hosted the New Zealanders on clay in the city of Florianopolis, which was absolutely no coincidence. Florianopolis, located on an island off Brazil's southern coast, is the home of Gustavo "Guga" Kuerten, who arrived in Paris last May with a low profile and reservations in a two-star hotel and left with the French Open title and a congratulatory fax from national icon Pelé.

When he finally returned to Florianopolis after Wimbledon, Kuerten was met by tens of thousands of well-wishers who lighted firecrackers and waved small pennants bearing the message "Valeu Guga" ("Well Done, Guga") as he made his way in a car from the airport to a reception in his honor at city hall.

"It was great to see that the people treated the French Open like one of Brazil's World Cup soccer matches," Kuerten said. "Everybody stopped when I was playing and started to watch the match and hoped I'd win. I felt that support when I got home, and it was really exciting."

It was less exhilarating to have to hire bodyguards, install a security gate in front of his family's home and change his telephone number to stop the incessant ringing. But such is the price of contemporary celebrity.

"I was surprised how instantly recognizable he was," said Kuerten's agent, Jorge Salkeld. "We went to a drive-up window, and the girls saw him and all came running out for autographs. He lent me his car, and as I drove around the city, people would honk at me. They knew it was his car."

All of which means that for Kuerten to play Davis Cup in his hometown and remain focused was quite a challenge. As he walked around the resort hotel where the tie was held, the autograph requests were incessant, and they weren't only from strangers eager to get close to a star (like the fellow surfers who had asked for his signature when he was dripping wet with board in hand on a Florianopolis beach).

"I probably knew one or two thousand of the five thousand people in the stands," Kuerten said

At twenty-six, Marc Rosset is the grand old man of the Swiss team, above, but he and his younger compatriots relished their victory over Korea and the chance to compete in the 1998 World Group. Alexander Volkov, opposite top, returned to Davis Cup after a two-year absence and knocked out Ion Moldovan of Romania, opposite bottom, in the fifth and decisive match to put Russia back in the World Group. Preceding pages: not just a clay-courter, Marcelo Rios, left, showed that he can dominate on grass, but Chile still lost to India 3-2. Mahesh Bhupathi, right, thrilled both himself and his country, securing a place in the 1998 World Group for India by coming back from two sets down to defeat Chile's Gabriel Silberstein in the fifth and decisive rubber.

Samba! Brazil treated the irrepressible Guga like one of its World Cup soccer stars.

In the presence of Brazil's most devoted fans, Gustavo Kuerten with Jaime Oncins, top right, jumped for joy as Brazil defeated New Zealand, 5-0, in his home town of Florianopolis. Opposite: life hasn't been the same for Gustavo Kuerten since winning Roland Garros, especially when playing Davis Cup at home in Brazil.

An unlikely hero, Belgium's Christophe van Garsse completed Belgium's victory over France to the delight of his teammates . . .

with a chuckle. "But it was a great experience for me to come back and play a professional tournament for the first time in front of my friends and family."

All the greater because Kuerten played superbly in Brazil's 5-0 sweep of the New Zealanders, who looked extremely homesick for Auckland and the sweet smell of freshly cut grass. In five rubbers, the Brazilians did not drop a set. Kuerten beat Alistair Hunt in the opening match 7-5, 6-3, 6-2; Fernando Meligeni beat Brett Steven 6-3, 7-5, 6-4 in the second. On Saturday, the team clinched the victory when Kuerten and partner Jaime Oncins annihilated Hunt and Steven—both very respectable doubles players—by the astonishing score of 6-0, 6-2, 6-0.

"We thought it would be a difficult match for us, but we hit every shot," Kuerten said. "We played unbelievable."

The good-natured Kuerten would appear to have his priorities right, which explains why he decided to nix the unveiling of a 4.3-meter statue of himself that a Brazilian press group had commissioned and planned to install on one of Florianopolis's main thoroughfares.

"They wanted to put it up, but my family and I said no," Kuerten said. "It's a little early, you know. I'm kind of just starting my career."

Après la deluge, it's Belgium

In Paris, there was never any talk of statues on the Rue de Rivoli, but the French Davis Cup team certainly experienced its own brushes with hero worship after winning the title so dramatically in Sweden in 1996. There had been a parade down the Champs-Elysées in an open car that drew throngs of supporters; there had been a visit to the Elysées palace to meet with president Jacques Chirac.

But eight months later, the French found themselves in a considerably less gratifying and infinitely less glamorous situation. They found themselves in Gand, Belgium, trying to save face and their spot in the World Group against their neighbors in what the French call "un match de barrages."

Despite their shared border, France and Belgium had not played each other in twenty-two years, and though the Belgians have had Davis Cup success in the past—reaching the Final in 1904 and the inter-zone final in 1953 and 1957—the French have certainly been the more significant force in the modern game.

They might have been the more significant force in Gand, too, if their number-one player Cedric Pioline had not strained his back stretching for a ball at 5-5 in the third set of his opening singles match against Johan van Herck while leading two sets to love. But this would be the tie in which France was seemingly made to pay for its recent good fortune in Davis Cup.

With captain Yannick Noah sporting new and large sideburns, the French team arrived in Gand with a new look of their own. Arnaud Boetsch was out with an injury (perhaps for the best considering his 1997 results). Guy Forget, a doubles mainstay in recent years, had retired. Joining Pioline and Forget's tightly wound former doubles partner Guillaume Raoux were Fabrice Santoro and Lionel Roux.

The Belgian team arrived with Filip Dewulf, who in June had become the first qualifier to reach the French Open semifinals, van Herck, Christophe van Garsse and Libor Pimek, a Czech-born doubles specialist. They also arrived with a great deal at stake. The top Belgian women—Sabine Appelmans and Dominique Van Roost—had enjoyed fine seasons, reaching the quarterfinals of the Australian Open and the semifinals of the Fed Cup. Now, the Belgian men wanted to capitalize on some of their sport's rising popularity.

Only two thousand fans had come over three days to watch their first Group One match in 1997 against Denmark, but there were approximately three thousand paying customers in Hall Eight of the Flanders Expo for the first day against the French.

The last time Santoro had been asked to play Davis Cup was in 1991. He was eighteen years old and won a decisive fifth rubber against Australia in the quarterfinals, played against Yugoslavia in the semifinals and then was not selected by Noah for the final. Even though French veterans Forget and Henri Leconte ended up upsetting the Americans, Santoro felt betrayed and his tennis soon reflected it. That psychological blow, along with injuries and the Darwinian nature of contemporary men's tennis, held him back for most of the 1990s. But after starting the 1997 season ranked 118, the crafty Frenchman with two-handed strokes off both wings worked himself back to 41 and back onto Noah's team.

"I really want to experience this again," he said.

Unfortunately, he would do little to justify his captain's renewed faith in the opening singles rubber against Dewulf, losing 6-1, 6-3, 6-3. After Pioline's strained back forced him to retire at 4-6, 2-6, 7-5, 4-1, the Belgians were up 2-0. Raoux, bespectacled and intense, would keep the French afloat, shoring up Santoro's confidence in the next day's doubles and lifting him to a four-set victory over Dewulf and Pimek. Raoux then routed Dewulf in the fourth rubber in straight sets on Sunday in relief of Pioline.

Logically, Santoro should have played van Herck to break the tie. But Noah had seen enough, and he replaced Santoro, conveniently suffering from what was termed "a sore shoulder," with Roux, who had never played a Davis Cup match in his life, much less a decisive rubber. Never before had a team competing in the World Group or the Qualifying Round used four different singles players in its four singles matches.

But Belgian captain Eduardo Masso was in a gambling mood as well. Instead of van Herck, who was suffering from a leg injury that was probably less fictional than Santoro's ailment, he chose the 173rd-ranked van Garsse, who proceeded to play as if he were ranked about one hundred and fifty spots higher.

One year earlier, a surgeon had told van Garsse that his tennis career was probably over after performing major surgery on his left knee. But like another muscular and considerably more famous left-hander from Austria, van Garsse would prove the doctors wrong. Against Roux, the explosive Belgian took risk after risk and found line after line, fighting off break points with second-serve aces and other audacious strokes and inspiring the fine French tennis writer Philippe Bouin of L'Equipe to label him "a Flemish Leconte."

"My strategy was to hit the ball as hard as possible," van Garsse said.

After qualifying at Wimbledon in 1997 and reaching the third round, van Garsse was on his merry, muscular way to qualifying his nation for the World Group with a 7-5, 6-4, 1-6, 6-2 victory and making France the first defending champion to be relegated since the World Group was launched in 1981.

Roux, the rookie, shed tears. Noah, the guru, called for a cigarette and offered up no regrets.

"You must accept victory and defeat in the same way," he explained. "You can't say we are gods when we win, and then send us up in flames when we lose."

Only two weeks later, a bit farther north in Europe, Noah was in the midst of another reggae-dancing, champagne-popping, ego-affirming celebration as captain of the victorious French women's team that defeated Holland to capture its first Fed Cup title. By taking on two jobs, Noah had proved slump-proof. But as a leader of men, there was no question that this had not been his year.

. . . and the despair of French captain Yannick Noah, bottom.

Boris Becker

BORIS BECKER'S 1997 DAVIS CUP CAMPAIGN was one of the most unusual in memory. It began in February with Becker declining to make the journey to Mallorca to face the Spaniards on clay. It ended with Becker taking control of the German team.

Detachment to involvement: Becker has marched to his own drummer since he became a national icon at the precocious age of seventeen by boom-booming his way to the Wimbledon title. Twelve years later, with his thirtieth birthday loom-looming like a signpost in the desert, the semi-retired Becker made it clear he would approach his second career with equal self-assurance.

There would be no apprenticeship under longtime German captain Niki Pilic's wing, as Becker's longtime rival Michael Stich had proposed in his unsuccessful bid to enter the Davis Cup fray. Instead, Becker decided to make the leap from player to senior administrator, nudging aside Pilic and paying him generously for the inconvenience.

The announcement was made on October 7, one day before the draw for the 1998 Davis Cup. The new German captain would be Becker's friend and former Davis Cup teammate Carl-Uwe Steeb. Becker would assume the title of team manager, but he was clearly the one with the influence and agenda. "I want to help Germany stay on the map in world tennis," said Becker, the player who put it there with help from Steffi Graf and, to a lesser degree, Stich.

But 1997 was the year Germany's troika of stars relinquished control on the court. Graf missed much of the season after knee surgery and, with the rapid ascension of Martina Hingis, looked uncertain to reassert her dominance if she returned. The sore-shouldered Stich retired at Wimbledon after losing in the semifinals to Cedric Pioline. One round earlier, in the midst of an injury-riddled season in which he never reached a final, Becker lost to Pete Sampras and informed his surprised opponent that he had just played his last match at Wimbledon: the verdant proving ground where he won in 1985, 1986 and 1989 and reached the final on four other occasions.

Though Becker entered the U.S. Open, he withdrew because of the death of his advisor Axel Meyer-Woelden, who succumbed to liver cancer in August. With his Grand Slam singles career behind him, Becker easily won both his singles rubbers in a 5-0 Qualifying Round romp over Mexico to improve his career Davis Cup singles record to a glittering 38-3.

With Germany's place in the World Group secure, Becker announced that he planned to play for Germany again in 1998. But it became clear that his plans were considerably more extensive. Becker already was busy overseeing the new junior team, which included rising star Nicolas Kiefer. And in mid-July, German Tennis Federation president Claus Stauder approached Becker privately about cementing ties with the federation and overseeing Davis Cup. Though Pilic's contract did not expire until September 1998, Stauder was convinced the transition should happen sooner not later. Pilic was soon a consultant, and Becker and Steeb were soon a team, although Becker is clearly in power.

"With Stich already stopping his career and Boris preparing to do so, it's a very important moment for German tennis," Stauder said. "We need to gain as much time as possible. I think with Boris as manager and Charlie as captain and with young players like Kiefer and Tommy Haas and Daniel Elsner coming up, this is a good situation now to start a new era in German tennis. But of course it's normal that we will need some time for that."

It was all rather surprising. After making rumblings about retiring with his family to sunny, apolitical Florida, Becker ultimately decided, like Yannick Noah, John Newcombe and scores of other former tennis stars, that he would remain involved in the sport that made his reputation and fortune. He plans to do more than evaluate and nurture talent. He plans to market Davis Cup in Germany and enlist sponsors. According to Stauder, even though Becker has not asked to be paid for his efforts, he has given an informal commitment of five years to the team. "I think this is the best thing that could have happened to the Davis Cup situation in Germany, but it is more than that," said Stauder. "What Boris wants to do is work from the base of the game to the top and give all his experience back to German tennis. He has changed a lot. If you would have discussed such matters with him even a year ago, he was a different person."

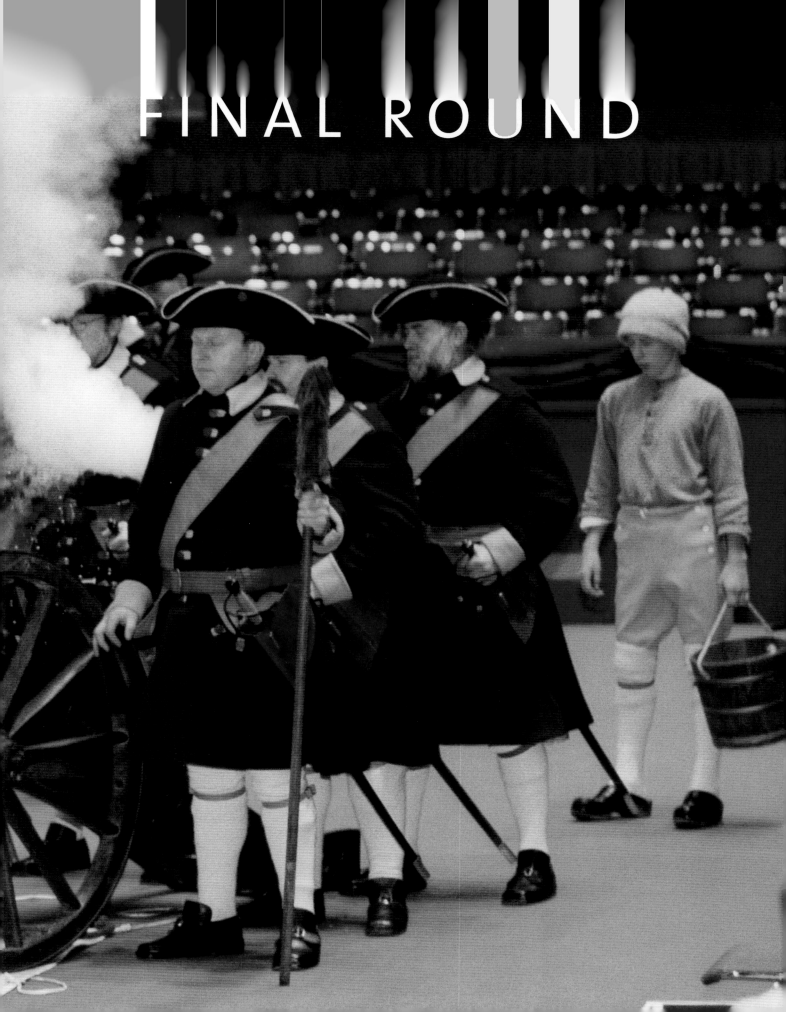

Ghösteborg? The Americans wonder

THE NIGHTS AND SCARVES WERE LONG; the ice and overcoats were thick.

The Davis Cup Final had returned to Sweden, but one only had to walk the frozen streets of Gothenburg in the days before the tie to see how much had changed in the last year.

Instead of hosting the sport's most prestigious team event in hard-scrabble surroundings near the Malmö docks in a converted factory, this Final would take place in Sweden's second largest city and second largest sports arena: the Scandinavium, which might not be worthy of an architectural prize but at least had the feel of a major venue.

The Swedish Association had purchased advertising space to promote the tie throughout Gothenburg, and the poster boys were Pete Sampras and Jonas Björkman. Sampras, pictured with an American flag draped around his torso in a climate where an American quilt would have been more appropriate, had not even deigned to play Davis Cup the year before. Björkman, pictured in the midst of smacking his much-improved forehand, had, in last year's stranger-than-fiction Final against the French, only played (and lost) the doubles, and when Swedish captain Carl-Axel Hageskog had to select a journeyman substitute to replace the injured Stefan Edberg in the decisive rubber, he picked Nicklas Kulti rather than his higher-ranked doubles partner, Björkman.

Benchwarmer to potential world-beater: It had been a heady ascension for Björkman, who had soared from sixty-nine in the rankings in January to four on the eve of the Final, and as he walked the frozen streets, the meaning of the huge posters was not lost on him.

"It was an unusual situation for me, but it was definitely nice because it showed that I've been coming maybe further than I expected," he said. "The good thing was that I felt ready for it. It's easier to be ready for it when you are twenty-five and have been around a little bit than when you are nineteen or twenty and it all happens so fast."

Björkman not only felt ready for stardom; he felt ready to upset the Americans. Three months earlier, after Sampras and Michael Chang had swept through a fine and cohesive Australian team in the semifinals, optimism had not been so pervasive in the Swedes's boisterous locker room, but recent events had changed their attitude. Chang, perhaps still reeling psychologically from his missed opportunity at the U.S. Open, had struggled mightily indoors throughout the fall and had lost five of his last six matches when he arrived in Gothenburg. One of those losses had come in straight sets against Björkman in the round-robin portion of the ATP Tour World Championship in Hannover, Germany.

Björkman's recent results had been nothing short of remarkable. After reaching his first Grand Slam semifinal at the U.S. Open, he had reached the semifinals in Stuttgart and the finals of the Paris Indoor before winning his nation's most prestigious tournament in Stockholm. Nor was he the only Swede in fine form. Magnus Larsson and Thomas Enqvist, who were locked in an amicable struggle for the team's second-singles spot, also had emitted flashes of brilliance in recent weeks.

But none of the Swedes had been as flashy as Sampras, who had won in Munich, Paris and Hannover, where he had been voted the best player of the Open Era by a panel of experts. However, the

Although the American fans cheered loyally, it was Sweden's supporters who had the most to smile about. Preceding pages: when the smoke cleared, Sweden had won a sixth Davis Cup title.

Tales from the crypt

In the 1984 Final in Gothenburg, number-one ranked John McEnroe and number two Jimmy Connors, always a reluctant Davis Cupper despite his deeply combative nature, made for strange bedfellows and a bad and bad-tempered team. The Swedes stunned them 4-1 on an indoor claycourt, clinching victory after only two days as Mats Wilander routed Connors; Henrik Sundstrom shocked McEnroe; and Anders Jarryd and the almost eighteen-year-old Edberg dealt McEnroe and longtime partner Peter Fleming their first and only Davis Cup doubles defeat.

"That's one of my best memories in my career," Stefan Edberg said. "Everybody on our team was young and full of enthusiasm. It was a new generation making its mark."

Edberg was no youngster when the Americans returned a decade later for a semifinal on a fast carpet. It was Tom Gullikson's first year as captain, and it did not end happily as the United States blew a 2-0 lead for only the second time in its long history. On the final day, Sampras, already number one in the world in 1994, strained a leg muscle and had to retire against Edberg, and then Martin was upset by Larsson in the decisive rubber. Larsson celebrated by leaping the net, and the Swedes went on to defeat Russia in the Final.

Americans still had no established Davis Cup doubles team, and Björkman and his henchmen felt that, even if Sampras won both his singles rubbers, their chances in the other three matches were excellent.

"With one week to go, we really believed," Björkman said.

The Americans were full of self-belief themselves, and on the eve of the opening matches, as they ate a memorable Thanksgiving dinner prepared by the squad's personal chef on the top floor of a tony Gothenburg restaurant, United States Tennis Association President Harry Marmion raised a glass and thanked the American supporters for coming to watch the team's victory. It was a bold statement: particularly in light of his nation's troubled past in Gothenburg.

The Americans held a convincing 7-2 advantage over the Swedes in head-to-head matches, but they were only 1-2 in this port city. Though they beat the Swedes on their first visit in 1978, they lost in the Scandinavium in 1984 and 1994 and on both occasions they had been favored to win.

"We're hoping the third time will be lucky because it certainly hasn't been a charmed city for us," said Gullikson, neglecting to revel in 1978. "We're planning to take care of 1994 and the ghost of 1984 at the same time."

Pete Sampras sounded less interested in exorcism and more interested in an exit visa. Even after a week of rest in Los Angeles, during which he said he hit for "an hour," he sounded disgruntled to be still playing in late November. "It's never going to end," he said of his season.

Asked if he could see a way for the schedule to be rearranged so that he would play Davis Cup every round, he shook his head. "It's just too much," he said. "When this week's over, I have literally four weeks off. I need to recuperate and get ready for Australia."

"And kiss his girlfriend," chimed in American player Jeff Tarango, in Gothenburg as a hitting partner.

"Yeah," said Sampras.

Despite his creeping ennui, Sampras still practiced brilliantly and enthusiastically—not always his hallmark—in the days leading up to the tie.

"I honestly thought that with Pete, we had two matches in our pocket," said Todd Martin. "And I figured with Michael's two matches and the doubles match, we'd certainly be able to snag one more."

And then there were none

One American star who did not come to Gothenburg was Jim Courier, who had torn a quadricep muscle in Asia shortly after the semifinal victory over the Australians. And when doubles player Alex O'Brien withdrew at the final hour because of a stress fracture in his foot and was replaced by Jonathan Stark, the Americans no longer had any holdovers from the team that had beaten the heat and some very good claycourters in Brazil in the first round.

"I love *esprit de corps*," Courier had said earlier in the year. "I wish we could get a group of five or six guys and say, 'This is our team,' and every time we went somewhere it was the same guys. I wish that was the case, because then you really develop it. You really get the camaraderie going, and the nations that don't have the options of players, they have that camaraderie because their players have to play every tie."

The Swedes, who travel, train and take meals in a pack for much of the year, definitely had camaraderie, but even they had not kept the same lineup from start to finish. By now, it was easy to forget that Björkman had skipped the opening tie against Switzerland. Much of the Swedish press was convinced that he had done so to protest being left on the bench against France while Kulti squandered three match points in the Final. Björkman had indeed felt slighted, and the slight was rendered more complex because of the existing antipathy between Hageskog and Björkman's coach Fredrik Rosengren, who both hail from the same Växjö tennis club. But Björkman insisted that he was not the sort to hold grudges.

"Of course, I was disappointed," he said. "If you're not disappointed that you didn't get to play in the Davis Cup Final then I think there is something wrong with you. But it was something I let go after a week."

The problem, according to Björkman, was his right knee, which had been swollen and irritated throughout the autumn of 1996. He had received a cortisone injection shortly after the Final but felt that he had missed too much practice time to commit to the first round. Hageskog, like the fourth estate, was not entirely convinced of Björkman's motives and let his own disappointment filter through publicly.

"The whole thing got a little bit exaggerated," Björkman said.

But as Björkman warmed up against Chang before the opening rubber of the Final, the Swedes were showing their customary unified front, and for anyone who relishes foreshadowing, there was plenty of it courtside in the form of Edberg, Sundstrom and assistant captain Jarryd—all seminal figures in the 1984 Final.

More important for the future of Swedish tennis were the 11,558 fans who had crowded into the sold-out Scandinavium. Despite the nation's remarkable legacy of tennis success, the sport has struggled to hold its audience throughout the 1990s. The Swedish public's indifference has not always been easy to comprehend—wasn't Edberg still a major threat to win majors in the nineties?—but it was very real.

"Tennis was, of course, pushed forward a great deal with Björn Borg, and even in the eighties tennis was very popular," Edberg once explained to L'Equipe. "Everybody watched the Davis Cup matches, even the old people, because it was a team event and maybe a lot of Swedes had that same mentality: a team mentality, working as a group. I'm sure it's because of this that tennis became as popular as soccer and hockey. The newspapers wrote big stories on you every time you got to the quarterfinals of a tournament. But in recent years the media coverage dropped off enormously."

When the Americans arrived for the semifinal in 1994, the Swedes only used half the Scandinavium and could not manage to sell it out, which was hardly an anomaly. The 1996 Davis Cup Final, Edberg's farewell event before retiring, was not even broadcast on one of Sweden's major networks. Instead, it was broadcast on a cable channel that was unavailable in many Swedish homes.

"We see no clear reason for the tennis slump," said Lena Berggren, an assistant to the general secretary at the Swedish Association. "Maybe it had to do with other sports giving us competition, like golf, which has begun drawing big crowds. But it all remains something of a mystery."

Björkman believes it had something to do with complacency. "I think everyone got quite satisfied; quite used to seeing the Swedes in the Final all the time or winning. I think they needed a few bad years to get back to appreciating it."

Others believe the relatively egalitarian Swedes rejected tennis because its players came across as pampered, overpaid profiteers who set up tax homes, if not real homes, in Monte Carlo. Still others, like Jarryd and Edberg, believe it was merely a question of riding out a cycle.

"You can't just get the same raw development." Jarryd said. "Sometimes the kids choose other sports, but if they see someone they think is a great athlete and a good guy, it makes them want to start. I think Jonas is a little bit like that now."

"This is a new tennis generation," Edberg said in Gothenburg. "It's new people and new faces and that's what people need sometimes. Tennis was down in general, but now it's picking itself up. That doesn't mean we don't have to work at it."

The Swedes did work at it before this Final. After being criticized in 1996 for overcatering to the corporate community, the association reached out this time to its core constituency and to the young and the true tennis believers. Hageskog wrote to all of Sweden's clubs asking for support for the Final, and just in case patriotism was not quite enough inspiration, club members were offered half-price tickets.

Apparently, Swedes appreciate a bargain as much as they appreciate Björkman's freshness and charisma because the Final was sold out weeks before the matches began. When they did begin, Sampras, Martin and Stark—all part of the losing 1994 American effort—must have had difficulty recognizing the arena that had been so somber and uninspiring during their last visit. This time, there were buff-and-blue-clad Swedes everywhere, many of them sporting conical striped hats made of felt that could have been lifted straight from the whimsical pages of a Dr. Seuss book.

There was even a drum-thumping, whistle-tooting Samba band in the arena's upper reaches that made one forget—if only temporarily—that the temperatures outside were flirting with zero. The French fans had shouted down the Swedes on the opening day of the 1996 Final, but the Americans, still digesting their turkey and stuffing and pumpkin soup, would have no such opportunity. "We are starting to climb out of the valley," Hageskog said.

This was the sixth Final in Sweden and the fourth in the Scandinavium. The only one the Swedes had lost here was in 1988 to Boris Becker and the Germans: a defeat Edberg still considers one of the biggest disappointments of his career. Surprisingly, this was only the second Final between the Swedes and Americans, the two most successful Davis Cup nations of the competition's new era. Since the World Group was formed in 1981, the only Final not to include Sweden or the United States was in 1993 when Germany defeated Australia. But improbably, the only time the Swedes and Americans both managed to reach the Final Round in the same year was in 1984.

What should have been a great rivalry had yet to realize its potential, but the mutual respect was clearly there, and in the week before the Final, Martin and Stark mingled easily with their Swedish rivals, and Gullikson greeted the Swedes cheerily as he crossed their paths at the practice court.

"For me personally, the Swedes are my favorite group of players outside North America," Martin said. "They are just a very easy-going group of guys. They enjoy what they do. They are incredibly competitive without letting it get in the way of their lives and being gentlemen."

Perhaps, but their treatment of each other is not always gentlemanly. The Swedes are devoted practical jokers, particularly Kulti, and Björkman is not the first or last to experience the unpleasant sensation caused by liniment finding its way unexpectedly into his underwear.

"You give one and receive one on this team," Björkman said. "There are a lot of things you have to be careful of. You make one mistake, and you're in trouble."

Speed against speed; strength against strength

There would be mistakes aplenty in the first rubber of the Final, as Björkman and Chang fought nerves and each other for the second time in two weeks. For Björkman, the stakes were very clear: beat Chang, or Sweden's chances of victory became remote. For Chang, who had Sampras as a safety net, the stakes were less sharply defined. But instead of swinging with confidence, the earnest and normally reliable American responded with one of his shakiest opening sets in memory.

That Björkman won it by the tight score of 7-5 only reflected his own level of anxiety. Chang managed to put just 28 percent of his first serves in play and double faulted six times. "Just a joke," said Chang, who also had nine more unforced errors than winners. About the only place he had consistent success on the medium-speed Taraflex surface was at the net, and Gullikson kept urging him forward on the changeovers.

Until the ATP World Championships in Hannover, Chang had never had difficulty handling Björkman, beating him in straight sets in their first three meetings, all on hardcourts. But now it seemed the Swede was getting inside his head, and not the other way around as is usual with the cerebral Chang.

"I knew it would be tough to beat Chang twice in a row, especially in big events," Björkman said. "But I still felt I had a good chance, because in Hannover, I felt he was the one who changed his game as the match went on, which meant he had more respect for my tennis than I had for his. That helped me a lot mentally."

Anyone who thinks modern indoor tennis is a stultifying affair dominated by the serve and played exclusively at a staccato pace has not watched Björkman play Chang. Two of the quickest men in tennis, both are capable of turning an opponent's would-be winners to their own advantage, and as the match wore on, both put their retrieving skills and raw athleticism to good use.

Chang would lift his game in the second set, winning it 6-1 as his service percentage and confidence climbed precipitously. He broke Björkman twice in that set and broke the Swede the first two times he served in the third set to take a 3-1 lead. But if any man, in the absence of Agassi, can return better than Chang, it is Björkman, and the American would prove incapable of holding his lead. With Chang serving at 3-2, 40-30, the two overachievers locked wills and reflexes in one of the finest points of this or any other year: a point in which Björkman scrambled and threw up a high lob that somehow traveled unscathed between two of the steel beams supporting the Scandinavium's lights.

It is well nigh impossible to convey the thrill of a high-velocity tennis exchange in print—oh, for a little interactivity—but Luddite readers deserve our best effort: Chang hit an overhead. Björkman twitched and slammed it back and then worked his way to net, where Chang hit one of his typically fine lobs over the Swede's backhand wing. Björkman leaped and somehow managed an acrobatic backhand overhead. Chang tried to pass him. Björkman hit a deft forehand angle volley. Chang sprinted toward the dying ball, hit a desperation forehand, went sprawling and never got to see the ball land long.

Instead, he got the pleasure of hearing approximately eleven thousand punch-drunk Swedes chanting "YOOOO-ness BYORK-man, YOOO-ness BYORK-man" as he walked back to serve. Chang did not know it yet, but he was about to lose that game and the match, dropping the final two sets 6-3, 6-3.

"In a sense, that was probably the turning point," Chang said. And in a sense, Waterloo was probably the turning point of the Napoleonic Wars.

There would be fourteen service breaks in the match, but none would have quite the same psychological effect as the one that followed that breathtaking exchange. The game's premier hustler had been outhustled.

"The funny thing is that almost the same thing happened in Hannover," Björkman said. "I won a point there on his serve where I was running all over at the end of the second set, and then I broke him. Everything has just been going my way lately, and a point like that gives you one more reason to feel positive."

Intensity. Jonas Björkman outhustled Michael Chang, the game's premier hustler.

For every Michael Chang (above) parry, Jonas Björkman (opposite) found the appropriate response.

As for Chang, a devout Christian who has often found inspiration in the biblical story of Job, it was clear that even he was reaching the outer limits of his patience.

"When did you last feel so disappointed that you weren't able to do yourself justice in a big match?" someone asked.

"Hard to say," he answered. "I think I've had disappointing times in my career. At this point, you know, I'm pretty far down there. I think it's never an easy thing to go through. Each day becomes difficult to pick yourself back up and go on and work hard. You know, I've tried to go on and work hard. I always feel like the Lord has his purpose for everything. It's just tough. I don't think it's any different for me. When you work hard, and you're still coming up short, still failing, it can get tough."

For anyone who has listened to Chang regularly over the years as he has resolutely reshaped his game in an attempt to win a second Grand Slam title after the 1989 French Open, this was despondent stuff indeed.

"I can't explain it; I wish I could," he said. "I wish I could tell you that I've had times where I was absolutely lazy and just didn't do anything; didn't work on my game. But it's not something I can tell you. If I knew the reason, I would fix it. Having lost this many matches, I would never go through that without making a change if I knew the answer."

The best answer for his second straight loss to Björkman came from Martin, one of the tour's more thoughtful men: "Jonas moves pretty close to as well as Michael, and he moves forward whereas Michael moves side to side. And I think in this day and age, if two guys move equally well and one guy is moving well inside the court, he's going to have better success than the guy moving well outside."

Sweden was now on the move with a 1-0 lead and, to celebrate, Björkman leaned forward and grabbed the toe of his right sneaker with his right hand and then pointed one finger in the air (don't try this at home). This awkward pose had become Björkman's trademark after big victories, and it came from a comedy routine created by a popular Swedish troupe called Galenskaparna, literally "the crazy makers." In the routine, the comedians grab their toes and do an ungainly walk they call the "Brusselstep" (didn't someone once say that tragedy was universal and comedy was local?).

Of course, all that really mattered was that Björkman and the Swedes, who saw and loved Galenskaparna live in Gothenburg before the Final, found meaning in this gesture, and that they were able to avoid serious injury while performing it.

"You've got to be a good athlete," Björkman conceded.

Tennis can be risky, too

With his sloping shoulders and duck-footed gait, Magnus Larsson does not look like much of an athlete, but Pete Sampras and many others know that the six-foot-four-inch Larsson's gangly appearance is utterly deceptive. If Larsson had been chosen ahead of Enqvist for the second singles spot, it was not because Hageskog was his personal coach, although that situation certainly left the door ajar for misinterpretation. It was because he had beaten Enqvist twice that autumn and outplayed him in practice and, lest one forget the essential, because he was the only person on earth who had beaten Sampras twice in 1997.

Those victories had come on clay in Monte Carlo and on a hardcourt in Indianapolis. Larsson also had beaten Sampras on carpet in the Final of the 1994 Grand Slam Cup when he was in the midst of climbing to a career-high number 10 in the rankings. That climb ended abruptly in mid-1995 when he broke his right foot in an exhibition, and his level of motivation has fluctuated wildly in recent years. But when roused, he remains one of his sport's most dangerous players, and not simply because of his huge serve and heavy forehand.

"He is incredibly well-balanced, and his control of the ball is exceptional," Martin said. "He plays like people played fifteen to twenty years ago with the drop shots and the little slices. He uses as close to all of the court as anybody these days."

Sampras, still the owner of a 6-3 career edge over the 25th-ranked Larsson, was not prepared to be quite so complimentary, but he was hardly surprised to hear Larsson's name announced at the draw.

"He moves well and has some good feel," Sampras said. "He's confident. He has beat me before, but I feel like I'm playing well. I just need to go out and do it."

Sampras would do just fine in the first set, winning it 6-3 with some typically glittering shotmaking. He appeared to be well within his large and intimidating comfort zone. But then, midway through the second set, he felt what he would later term "a grab" in his left calf.

"It was almost like a cramp," Sampras said. "I figured it would go away as I continued to play."

He figured wrong. Trailing 4-3 with his service to come in the second set, Sampras received treatment on the changeover from U.S. Davis Cup team trainer, Todd Snyder, who is also Sampras's personal trainer. Two games later, trailing 5-4 with his service to follow, he took an injury timeout and had the calf wrapped tightly. He received treatment again at 6-5 and then held serve to force a tiebreaker, saving two set points along the way.

But Sampras, who throughout his brilliant career has often had a harder time with his fragile physique than with his rapidly evolving cast of rivals, was running out of tricks. Trailing 1-0, he tried one of his signature leaping overheads—a shot he used to great psychological effect against Patrick Rafter in the semifinals. This time, he ended up looking like a weekend warrior, shanking the overhead long. He would win the next point but would win no more in the breaker, losing it 7-1.

"I was pretty much bluffing at that point," Sampras said. "Basically it was hurting whenever I put weight on it, and I put most of my weight on my left leg when I serve."

Sampras swallowed an anti-inflammatory pill as he sat down after the second set, but after missing a forehand long to lose his serve in the opening game of the third, he began moving almost as slowly as an Ingmar Bergman film, and at 2-1, he walked up to chair umpire Andreas Egli of Switzerland and announced that the match and his season were over.

"It didn't make sense to continue the way I was feeling," said Sampras, who, it would turn out, had suffered a small muscle tear in his calf, not to mention an equally painful case of déjà vu.

On his last visit to the Scandinavium in 1994, he had hobbled off court with an injured hamstring. This time, he hobbled off early again, thereby adding one more skeleton to a closet that is becoming increasingly difficult to close.

Perhaps this seemingly innocuous city—once voted Sweden's friendliest by other Swedes—really was cursed. Not only was Göteborg devilishly difficult for Americans to pronounce; it was also hazardous to their health. Perhaps it would have been better if the Swedes had not decided to rebuild after the Danes burned the place to the ground in the sixteenth century.

"They've got us under a spell or something," said U.S. team physician George Fareed. "It really is eerie."

What Fareed probably did not realize was that Stockholm, not Gothenburg, was the Swedes's first choice as host city for this Final. But when the Globe arena in Stockholm turned out to be booked, the Swedes settled for the Scandinavium.

The only person who had defeated Pete Sampras (top) twice in 1997 was Magnus Larsson (bottom) who made it three victories in Gothenburg. Following pages: trainer Todd Snyder attends to Pete Sampras as referee Bill Gilmour and Tom Gullikson look on.

"It might not have been the plan," Björkman said, "but we knew that mentally, it was to our advantage."

Now, after only one day of tennis, the Scandinavium was beginning to smell suspiciously like dead rubber, and the only ones holding their noses were the Americans. The Swedes had been waiting twelve months for their chance at Davis Cup redemption, and now it was well within their reach.

When they had lost to the French in the final set on the final day in Malmö, the Swedish players had dutifully sat through a very late and long official dinner and then gathered dejectedly in their hotel, sipping beers in the middle of the night and commiserating. Larsson, only a practice partner in 1996, said "we talked until we were too drunk to talk anymore." According to Björkman, Larsson was exaggerating slightly, but everyone agreed the disappointment was palpable.

"Last year's Final was a great match and a great thing for tennis all over the world, so we were happy to be involved in that, but on the other hand all we needed was one more point," Hageskog said. "It seems like me and the boys were determined to take the Cup this year. It was more of a feeling than anything spoken. I wrote a letter to all the players for Christmas last year, and I explained that I was proud of them and that I thought we were going to get revenge. We didn't really speak much more about it, but I have seen in the matches this year that the boys were very determined."

Despite the ominous fact that no Swedish team had ever blown a 2-0 Davis Cup lead and no American team had erased one in sixty-three years, some of the visitors were still determined, too. None more than Justin Gimelstob, the twenty-year-old New Jerseyite whose power game is still a work in progress but whose self-confidence and outrageous sense of humor are not. Gimelstob had been a practice partner with the United States for much of the season and had actually drawn Australian captain John Newcombe's ire in the semifinals for his vocal and occasionally ill-timed exuberance in the stands. On Friday night in the Americans' team room at their hotel, Gimelstob slapped on a recording of the song "Tub Thumping," cranked up the volume and resumed being exuberant.

When the song was over, he walked out into the hallway and started screaming to no one in particular, "YOU THINK IT'S OVER? NO WAY. IT'S NOT OVER. THEY SAY IT'S IMPROBABLE. NO WAY."

"We were absolutely dying of laughter," Martin said.

Unfortunately for the Americans, young Gimelstob turned out to be a better performer than prognosticator.

A thumping without the tub

Without Sampras, Gullikson had to use Stark with Martin in Saturday's doubles against Björkman and Kulti, one of the world's best teams and finalists at the U.S. Open three months earlier. Martin and Stark can both play excellent doubles. Stark and his regular American partner Rick Leach, who had lost to Jacco Eltingh and Paul Haarhuis in the quarterfinals in Newport Beach, had just won the ATP Tour World Doubles Championship. But doubles is no exact science, and two skilled players do not necessarily form a fine team, especially not in a hurry. Martin and Stark had played only a handful of matches together, and their only previous Cup experience together was a straight-set loss to Björkman and Edberg in the 1995 semifinals.

Sweden's only real concern all week had been Kulti's chronically sore back but that had stopped nagging him by Wednesday. Doubles has long been a Swedish strength with players like Wilander, Jarryd and Edberg and though Björkman plans on playing less doubles in 1998 so he can focus on sin-

Doubles jeopardy

Bob Lutz and Stan Smith. John McEnroe and Peter Fleming. Ken Flach and Robert Seguso. Rick Leach and Jim Pugh. It once seemed that the supply of excellent American Davis Cup doubles teams was inexhaustible, but the pipeline has gone dry and the drilling has begun to look increasingly desperate.

For a player who had more success in doubles than singles, American captain Tom Gullikson ironically has proved incapable of cultivating a reliable combination in his four-year turn at the helm. In its last thirty-two ties, the United States is 19-0 when it wins the doubles and 7-6 when it does not.

In April 1997, frustrated USTA president Harry Marmion independently and quite extemporaneously floated the idea of creating a bonus pool to encourage Americans to play together. But that proposition turned out to be catchy rhetoric, not concrete policy, and after all, weren't Leach and Jonathan Stark already playing together?

"The problem is that most of our top players don't play doubles at all," said Gullikson, who used four different teams in 1997—one for each round— and had to sit by and watch all of them lose.

gles, neither he nor Kulti had any problem focusing on Saturday. With a 2-0 lead, the two free-swingers were able to swing even more freely and the consistent force of their returns and speed of their reactions ultimately proved too much for the Americans, particularly Martin, who often looked like he was playing at a more leisurely pace than the three other frenetic men on court.

"Starkie was serving big and the ball was coming back twice as fast," Gullikson said. "If you don't have unbelievably quick hands and are not really ready to cover that middle, the ball can get by you a little quickly and that's what was happening out there to Todd."

The Swedes took firm hold of the match at 4-4 in the first set, when the Americans proved incapable of holding a 40-0 lead on Stark's serve. Björkman earned the first break of the match by slamming a backhand return off a second serve that landed—as most great doubles returns should—at Stark's feet. Björkman then served out the set.

"All of a sudden we were playing from behind, and we were behind enough," Gullikson said.

As the Swedes won the second set, 6-4, someone in the American cheering section waved a made-for-television sign that read, "HI MOM SEND MONEY." "Players" would have been more appropriate.

The Americans kept doggedly at it, switching sides before the third set (which probably boosted the Swedes' confidence as much as theirs). But the rest of the match, like this Final as a whole, would prove anticlimactic, and Björkman was soon serving for the Cup at 5-4. He saved one break point with a first serve that Martin knocked long, another with an ace and a third when Martin hit yet another backhand reflex volley out. The Swede, reputed to be shaky under pressure until this season, would not have to save a fourth, and when he closed out the match with another ace up the middle in the ad-court, he was airborne.

"You need to jump high because there's no better feeling," he said.

By the time he landed, Kulti, a Davis Cup sob story no longer, was already rushing toward him. And before Björkman had time even to think about reaching down and grabbing the toe of his sneaker, the two friends were locked in a very public embrace.

"For a time, I was sad and angry about last year's Final, and I kept thinking about how I should have played those three match points," Kulti said. "But now I have stopped thinking about it. It's a wonderful thing to win the Davis Cup in Sweden. It's the sort of thing you dream about when you practice as a small child."

That was undoubtedly true, but it was also true that the Swedish celebration was not as emotional as it would have been if the world's best player had been across the net instead of in a Gothenburg hotel suite with his torn left calf wrapped and elevated and his mind, at least, temporarily on reform.

"The season is too long; way too long," Sampras said. "I've always felt that way, and I've told the tour. When you're sitting around today watching the Swedes win, it makes me think I should be out there healthy and playing. You get a little bit angry when you think about it."

"I want to play this game for five or seven more years and play it healthy," he added. "I think I got this injury from overplaying and not giving myself enough time to rest. This is my fourth trip to Europe in the last month and a half. I sort of would like to have five or six or seven weeks off to enjoy my year and recuperate mentally and physically."

The hyperactive Björkman played with so much verve in Gothenburg that it seemed he was starting his season not ending it, but even he agreed with Sampras. "I think it would be good if we could get everything finished by the end of October or first week of November," he said. "I think that way you might see some of us around for a lot longer."

Although Tom Gullikson fiddled with his doubles line-up all year, the team did not produce a victory in 1997. Putting last year's loss to France behind them, Jonas Björkman (top right) and Nicklas Kulti (top left) celebrated this year's victory over the United States while Jonathan Stark and Todd Martin were left to ponder what might have been.

Tennis historians never will know how this Final would have unfolded if Sampras had stayed around longer. All they will know is that the Swedes won as convincingly as Davis Cup allows after sweeping the last two meaningless singles matches on Sunday. Björkman beat Stark 6-1, 6-1 despite spending some of the night vomiting with a stomach ailment that he insisted had nothing to do with the Swedes's celebration at Invito, their watering hole of choice on Gothenburg's main thoroughfare. Larsson then defeated Chang, who played like the match still mattered, 7-6 (7-4), 6-7 (6-8), 6-4.

"To be honest, I think I would have won that match even if the score was 2-2," said Larsson, before joking that if he had Björkman's feet he could be ranked even higher than number four. "I'm going back home to jump rope," he said.

Larsson would not stay in a jovial mood for long. The day after he returned to Växjö, a bomb exploded in the middle of the night and destroyed the vehicle he had rented and parked in front of his house. Though the Swedish police announced that they did not believe Larsson was being targeted, the explosion surely must have dimmed the pleasant afterglow of a big victory.

Sweden's sixth Davis Cup title was indeed a big victory. Statistics, as ITF president Brian Tobin joked later, might be like a bikini in that they reveal what's interesting and hide what's important, but there was no hiding this: Sweden's 5-0 victory made it the first team to sweep the United States in a Cup tie since the 1973 Final, when a pair of all-time greats from Australia, Rod Laver and John Newcombe, vented their frustration at being pointlessly excluded from previous Cups because they were contract professionals.

"I said in the beginning that there were going to be five tough matches," said Hageskog. "But I didn't really think of winning them all. We had the luck on our side. It was a pity for Pete and for the U.S. team that he was injured."

Despite Björkman's remarkable progress this year at age twenty-five, it is safe to say there were no all-time greats on this Swedish team. No Borgs. No Wilanders. No Edbergs. What these Swedes had was unity, a noun frequently in short supply in the relentlessly individualistic microcosm of men's tennis. As if to remind everyone how tightly knit the Swedes were, Sampras chose to fly home to Tampa on Sunday morning as Stark and Chang prepared to play for pride and country. His early departure, injured calf or not, did not sit well with all the Americans who remained in Gothenburg.

It is odd that Sampras, so attuned and attached to the tradition of the Grand Slam events and to the Australian champions like Laver, should be comparatively tone deaf to the Davis Cup, which the great Australians treasured and is nearly as rich in history. Sampras says he enjoys Davis Cup but did not grow up watching it and reveling in it like he did Wimbledon or the U.S. Open, and he made it clear before he flew home for rehabilitation that he believes camaraderie is overrated in this team event.

"It's tennis; it's one-on-one," he said. "It's me against Larsson and Björkman against Chang. That's the way I look at Davis Cup. The fact that the Swedish guys and Australian guys being together all year makes a difference, I don't buy that."

The Swedes are much less skeptical consumers. How else to explain that their country now has won just as many Cups (five) as the United States since the World Group began in 1981 and with 270 million fewer inhabitants?

"Since 1983, we've been in the semifinals of the World Group every year but two and I think we've been winning so many matches because of our team spirit." Björkman said. "We are always pushing for each other, and no matter who is playing, the guy on the bench is doing as much as he can to help."

"We believe in Davis Cup," said Edberg, who traveled to Sweden to watch all four of his former

The level of play was as high as if the rubber were live but, at the end, Magnus Larsson (top) completed Sweden's 5-0 defeat of the United States by beating Michael Chang in the fifth and final match. Following pages: the triumphant Swedish team.

teammates' ties in 1997. "We work hard for it, and we give it more priority than other nations do. It is just about sacrifice."

The Americans have not always sacrificed in recent years, losing early in 1993 and 1996 because their best players were more interested in chasing ranking points. But in this case, Gullikson had his strongest singles players available and willing and still lost. The only thing the Americans won in Sweden was the fast-serve contest: Stark smacked one at 129.9 miles per hour.

"I came here with the idea of exorcising all the ghosts of Gothenburg's past," Gullikson said, shaking his head. "Instead, we have another nightmare."

Nightmares have slowly become the rule for the Americans in Davis Cup. This one can certainly be attributed to ill fortune, but some distant day, people are going to look at the record book, scratch their noggins and wonder why from 1993 to 1997—the five years Sampras reigned supreme over men's tennis—his nation won only one team title and Sweden won two.

"For the most part, the guys who play for the U.S. are individuals," Martin said. "They go out on the court. They're doing their job, and they realize it's a team competition, but they take the success and the failure personally. In some ways that's good, but I think it's also extremely important in Davis Cup to realize that you are competing for others as much as for yourself."

That realization can make you better. Just ask Patrick Rafter, or Omar Camporese, or Leander Paes, or the scores of other weekend patriots from 1900 until now who have found that embracing a collective goal can make that down-the-line forehand or tight angle volley or pressurized second serve just a little bit easier to hit.

The material rewards may not be as great as those for winning at the All England Club or Stade Roland Garros or in some converted showroom in Hannover, but there are rewards. And on Saturday night, as the Swedes were driven away from the Scandinavium to start celebrating, they passed some parked cars. Snow had fallen throughout the day, covering the vehicles with a thick layer of white. And on three successive windshields, some giddy Gothenburg youngsters had used their fingers to write three suddenly popular names in the moist canvas of the snow: "JONAS," "NICKLAS," "MAGNUS."

The World Group

Davis Cup champions since the beginning of the World Group in 1981

1981 United States
1982 United States
1983 Australia
1984 Sweden
1985 Sweden
1986 Australia
1987 Sweden
1988 Germany
1989 Germany
1990 United States
1991 France
1992 United States
1993 Germany
1994 Sweden
1995 United States
1996 France
1997 Sweden

Jonas Björkman

IT WAS SLIGHTLY AFTER 4 P.M. on the second day of the Davis Cup Final. The sun had already dropped below the horizon in Gothenburg, but Jonas Björkman was rising. The elastic, enthusiastic Swede with the bowed legs and bionic reflexes had just clinched his nation's sixth Davis Cup title with an ace, and now he was leaping toward the ceiling of the sold-out Scandinavium, free of pressure, free of the Americans and free of the shadow of any other Swedish tennis player.

This might have been Pete Sampras's year, but this was Björkman's long weekend. The man who can make his peers double over with laughter with his off-Broadway impersonations of John McEnroe, Stefan Edberg, Boris Becker and others was no longer an affable, unthreatening sideshow. He was the world's fourth-ranked singles player and the main reason the Swedish team was once again holding hands in a long, thin line and bowing triumphantly to the crowd.

"To be perfectly honest, I think Jonas is an overachiever," said Todd Martin. "Not to say that he isn't talented, but two or three years ago, if you would have asked anybody if Björkman could be in the top five, they probably would have said no."

The primary reason was Björkman's forehand, which had a nagging habit of breaking down under pressure. In 1997, after hours upon hours of drilling, that weakness became a weapon, but that technical leap only begins to explain how Björkman leaped sixty-five places in the rankings in eleven months. This was also the year Björkman began working with a psychologist to remove some of the knots in his stomach; the year he switched to a longbody racquet in an attempt to improve his serve; the year he invited his father Lars to stop delivering mail and start traveling with him to provide emotional support, and the year he inserted three strategic three-week breaks into his otherwise grueling schedule to give himself time to recharge his brain and body.

If he were a laboratory rat, scientists would have gleefully pronounced the experiment a success, and for anyone who watched his increasingly cocksure tennis throughout 1997, Björkman's glee was palpable, too. Always a spectacular shotmaker, he now seemed even more convinced that he could will small tennis balls through small gaps.

"He's so confident and playing so well, it's almost scary at times," said Stefan Edberg immediately after the Final.

Björkman will tell you that he was shy and plagued by self-doubt as a child. Unlike his Davis Cup teammates Magnus Larsson, Thomas Enqvist and Nicklas Kulti, he was not considered a top professional prospect as a junior, but that was, in part, because he was not just a tennis player. Lars Björkman had played second division hockey in Sweden and his son juggled hockey and soccer along with tennis until the age of fifteen and might well have tried skating for a living if he had been physically stronger.

"Before, I could use my speed and stick to my advantage, but then the other guys just started taking me out with their bodies," he said.

And so it would be tennis, a sport he began playing regularly at the age of eight in Växjö and a sport that became even more attractive two years later when Mats Wilander, a member of the same Växjö tennis club as Björkman, won the 1982 French Open.

But Wilander was not the first Swedish tennis idol. That honor belonged to Björn Borg, and when Borg telephoned Björkman during the Monte Carlo Open in 1996 and invited him to dinner, Björkman was thrilled and immediately called one of the principality's finer restaurants for a reservation, dropping Borg's name liberally in the process. But when he arrived with his Swedish teammates in tow, he found the table waiting but no Borg. The impressionist had fallen victim to another impressionist, longtime Borg friend and former touring pro Peter Lundgren. And his teammates were roaring with laughter.

"You should listen to Lundgren," Björkman said, still chuckling at himself two years later. "He's better than Borg at being Borg."

Björkman, no Grand Slam titles to his credit, cannot say the same, but he was better than any other Swede in 1997 and far better than any American in Gothenburg.

World Group

FIRST ROUND
February 7–9

USA defeated Brazil 4-1, Ribeirao Preto, BRA
MaliVai Washington (USA) d. Gustavo Kuerten (BRA) 3-6 7-6(6) 7-6(3) 6-3
Jim Courier (USA) d. Fernando Meligeni (BRA) 3-6 6-1 6-4 4-6 6-4
Kuerten/Jaime Oncins (BRA) d. Alex O'Brien/Richey Reneberg (USA) 6-2 6-4 7-5
Jim Courier (USA) d. Gustavo Kuerten (BRA) 6-3 6-2 5-7 7-6(11)
Alex O'Brien (USA) d. Fernando Meligeni (BRA) 7-5 7-6(4)

Netherlands defeated Romania 3-2, Bucharest, ROM
Adrian Voinea (ROM) d. Paul Haarhuis (NED) 4-6 6-1 6-3 6-3
Andrei Pavel (ROM) d. Jan Siemerink (NED) 6-2 6-1 4-6 6-4
Jacco Eltingh/Paul Haarhuis (NED) d. Ion Moldovan/Razvan Sabau (ROM) 7-6(4) 6-4 6-3
Jan Siemerink (NED) d. Adrian Voinea (ROM) 7-6(6) 5-7 6-7(3) 7-6(8) 6-4
Paul Haarhuis (NED) d. Andrei Pavel (ROM) 6-3 6-1 6-2

Australia defeated France 4-1, Sydney, AUS
Patrick Rafter (AUS) d. Cedric Pioline (FRA) 3-6 6-7(5) 6-4 7-5 6-4
Mark Woodforde (AUS) d. Arnaud Boetsch (FRA) 6-4 6-4 6-3
Todd Woodbridge/Mark Woodforde (AUS) d. Guy Forget/Guillaume Raoux (FRA) 7-6(6) 6-4 6-3
Sandon Stolle (AUS) d. Cedric Pioline (FRA) 7-6(3) 6-4
Arnaud Boetsch (FRA) d. Patrick Rafter (AUS) 4-6 6-4 7-6(5)

Czech Republic defeated India 3-2, Pribram, IND
Petr Korda (CZE) d. Mahesh Bhupathi (IND) 6-3 6-7(2) 6-1 6-2
Leander Paes (IND) d. Jiri Novak (CZE) 6-2 6-3 6-7(5) 6-3
Bhupathi/Paes (IND) d. Martin Damm/Korda (CZE) 7-6(7) 6-3 6-4
Petr Korda (CZE) d. Leander Paes (IND) 5-7 6-3 6-4 6-1
Jiri Novak (CZE) d. Mahesh Bhupathi (IND) 6-1 6-4 6-3

Italy defeated Mexico 4-1, Rome, ITA
Omar Camporese (ITA) d. Alejandro Hernandez (MEX) 2-6 6-0 6-4 7-5
Renzo Furlan (ITA) d. Luis Herrera (MEX) 3-6 6-1 6-2 6-1
Diego Nargiso/Stefano Pescosolido (ITA) d. Hernandez/Leonardo Lavalle (MEX) 6-1 4-6 7-6(7) 6-3
Renzo Furlan (ITA) d. Alejandro Hernandez (MEX) 6-2 6-3
Luis Herrera (MEX) d. Omar Camporese (ITA) 2-6 6-3 6-4

Spain defeated Germany 4-1, Mallorca, ESP
Carlos Moya (ESP) d. Marc-Kevin Goellner (GER) 6-4 6-3 6-3
Albert Costa (ESP) d. Hendrik Dreekmann (GER) 6-4 6-1 6-4
Mark-Kevin Goellner/David Prinosil (GER) d. Alex Corretja/Carlos Costa (ESP) 6-2 6-2 6-3
Carlos Moya (ESP) d. Hendrik Dreekmann (GER) 6-4 6-4 7-5
Albert Costa (ESP) d. Mark-Kevin Goellner (GER) 2-6 7-6(5) 6-1

South Africa defeated Russia 3-1, Durban, RSA
Marcos Ondruska (RSA) d. Andrei Chesnokov (RUS) 7-6(2) 6-3 3-6 4-6 7-5
Wayne Ferreira (RSA) d. Andrei Cherkasov (RUS) 7-5 6-3 3-6 4-6 8-6
Ellis Ferreira/Grant Stafford (RSA) d. Cherkasov/Andrei Olhovskiy (RUS) 6-2 3-6 6-0 6-2
Andrei Chesnokov (RUS) d. Wayne Ferreira (RSA) 6-2 6-7(5) 6-2
Marcos Ondruska (RSA) vs Andrei Cherkasov (RUS) not played

Sweden defeated Switzerland 4-1, Lulea, SWE
Marc Rosset (SUI) d. Magnus Larsson (SWE) 7-6(3) 3-6 6-4 4-6 1311
Thomas Enqvist (SWE) d. Lorenzo Manta (SUI) 7-6(4) 7-6(9) 6-2
Nicklas Kulti/Mikael Tillstrom (SWE) d. Lorenzo Manta/Marc Rosset (SUI) 5-7 6-4 6-3 5-7 6-4
Thomas Enqvist (SWE) d. Marc Rosset (SUI) 6-3 6-2 3-6 6-2
Magnus Larsson (SWE) d. Ivo Heuberger (SUI) 3-6 6-4 6-2

QUARTERFINAL ROUND
April 4–6

USA defeated Netherlands 4-1, Newport Beach, CA, USA
Andre Agassi (USA) d. Sjeng Schalken (NED) 7-6(6) 6-4 7-6(2)
Jim Courier (USA) d. Jan Siemerink (NED) 4-6 4-6 6-1 7-6(4) 6-3
Jacco Eltingh/Paul Haarhuis (NED) d. Rick Leach/Jonathan Stark (USA) 6-4 6-4 3-6 6-3
Andre Agassi (USA) d. Jan Siemerink (NED) 3-6 36 6-3 6-3 6-3
Jonathan Stark (USA) d. Sjeng Schalken (NED) 6-4 6-0

Australia defeated Czech Republic 5-0, Adelaide, AUS
Patrick Rafter (AUS) d. Martin Damm (CZE) 6-1 7-6(7) 6-4 6-4
Mark Philippoussis (AUS) d. David Rikl (CZE) 6-1 6-4 2-6 6-4
Todd Woodbridge/Mark Woodforde (AUS) d. Martin Damm/David Rikl (CZE) 4-6 6-1 7-5 6-4
Mark Philippoussis (AUS) d. Martin Damm (CZE) 6-4 6-2
Patrick Rafter (AUS) d. David Rikl (CZE) 7-6(13) 0-6 6-2

Italy defeated Spain 4-1, Pesaro, ITA
Omar Camporese (ITA) d. Carlos Moya (ESP) 6-7(8) 6-7(4) 6-1 6-3 6-3
Renzo Furlan (ITA) d. Albert Costa (ESP) 4-6 6-3 6-4 6-4
Camporese/Diego Nargiso (ITA) d. Francisco Roig/Javier Sanchez (ESP) 5-7 7-6(0) 6-2 7-6(5)
Carlos Moya (ESP) d. Marzio Martelli (ITA) 7-6(5) 4-6 6-3
Omar Camporese (ITA) d. Albert Costa (ESP) 6-2 3-6 6-4

Sweden defeated South Africa 3-2, Vaxjo, SWE
Thomas Enqvist (SWE) d. Grant Stafford (RSA) 7-5 2-6 6-4 6-1
Wayne Ferreira (RSA) d. Jonas Bjorkman (SWE) 6-3 6-4 2-6 7-6(3)
Bjorkman/Nicklas Kulti (SWE) d. David Adams/Ellis Ferreira (RSA) 7-5 2-6 6-4 6-7(6) 6-2
Wayne Ferreira (RSA) d. Thomas Enqvist (SWE) 6-4 6-4 6-4
Jonas Bjorkman (SWE) d. Grant Stafford (RSA) 3-6 6-0 3-6 6-2 6-2

SEMIFINAL ROUND
September 19–21

USA defeated Australia 4-1, Washington, DC, USA
Michael Chang (USA) d. Patrick Rafter (AUS) 6-4 16 6-3 6-4
Pete Sampras (USA) d. Mark Philippoussis (AUS) 6-1 6-2 7-6(5)
Todd Woodbridge/Mark Woodforde (AUS) d. Todd Martin/Sampras (USA) 3-6 7-6(5) 6-2 6-4
Pete Sampras (USA) d. Patrick Rafter (AUS) 6-7(6) 6-1 6-1 6-4
Michael Chang (USA) d. Mark Philippoussis (AUS) 7-6(5) 7-6(2)

Sweden defeated Italy 4-1, Norrkoping, SWE
Jonas Bjorkman (SWE) d. Omar Camporese (ITA) 6-7(5) 6-3 6-2 3-6 6-3
Renzo Furlan (ITA) d. Thomas Enqvist (SWE) 3-6 6-3 6-4 3-6 6-3
Jonas Bjorkman/Nicklas Kulti (SWE) d. Omar Camporese/Diego Nargiso (ITA) 6-1 6-1 6-2
Jonas Bjorkman (SWE) d. Renzo Furlan (ITA) 4-6 6-4 6-0 6-4
Thomas Enqvist (SWE) d. Omar Camporese (ITA) 6-3 6-7(5) 6-3

FINAL ROUND
November 28–30

Sweden defeated USA 5-0, Gothenburg, SWE
Jonas Bjorkman (SWE) d. Michael Chang (USA) 7-5 1-6 6-3 6-3
Magnus Larsson (SWE) d. Pete Sampras (USA) 3-6 7-6(1) 21 ret;
Jonas Bjorkman/Nicklas Kulti (SWE) d. Todd Martin/Jonathan Stark (USA) 6-4 6-4 6-4
Jonas Bjorkman (SWE) d. Jonathan Stark (USA) 6-1 6-1
Magnus Larsson (SWE) d. Michael Chang (USA) 7-6(4) 6-7(6) 6-4

QUALIFYING ROUND FOR 1998 WORLD GROUP
September 19-21

Zimbabwe defeated Austria 3-2, Harare, ZIM
Byron Black (ZIM) d. Gilbert Schaller (AUT) 6-3 6-2 6-1
Thomas Muster (AUT) d. Wayne Black (ZIM) 6-3 6-0 6-4
Byron Black/Wayne Black (ZIM) d. Georg Blumauer/Gerald Mandl (AUT) 7-5 6-4 6-3
Thomas Muster (AUT) d. Byron Black (ZIM) 3-6 6-3 2-6 6-3 6-1
Wayne Black (ZIM) d. Gerald Mandl (AUT) 5-7 6-3 6-3 6-0

Brazil defeated New Zealand 5-0, Florianopolis, BRA
Gustavo Kuerten (BRA) d. Alistair Hunt (NZL) 7-5 6-3 6-2
Fernando Meligeni (BRA) d. Brett Steven (NZL) 6-3 7-5 6-4
Gustavo Kuerten/Jaime Oncins (BRA) d. Alistair Hunt/Brett Steven (NZL) 6-0 6-2 6-0
Gustavo Kuerten (BRA) d. Brett Steven (NZL) 6-1 6-0
Andre Sa (BRA) d. Alistair Hunt (NZL) 6-2 6-2

India defeated Chile 3-2, New Delhi, IND
Leander Paes (IND) d. Gabriel Silberstein (CHI) 6-3 6-2 6-2
Marcelo Rios (CHI) d. Mahesh Bhupathi (IND) 6-2 3-6 6-3 6-4
Bhupathi/Paes (IND) d. Nicolas Massu/Rios (CHI) 3-6 6-3 6-4 6-7(3) 6-3
Marcelo Rios (CHI) d. Leander Paes (IND) 6-7(5) 6-4 6-0 7-6(3)
Mahesh Bhupathi (IND) d. Gabriel Silberstein (CHI) 6-7(4) 4-6 6-4 6-4 6-3

Belgium defeated France 3-2, Gent, BEL
Filip Dewulf (BEL) d. Fabrice Santoro (FRA) 6-1 6-3 6-3
Johan Van Herck (BEL) d. Cedric Pioline (FRA) 4-6 2-6 7-5 41 ret
Guillaume Raoux/Fabrice Santoro (FRA) d. Filip Dewulf/Libor Pimek (BEL) 5-7 7-5 7-5 6-1
Guillaume Raoux (FRA) d. Filip Dewulf (BEL) 6-3 6-4 7-5
Christophe Van Garsse (BEL) d. Lionel Roux (FRA) 7-5 6-4 1-6 6-2

Germany defeated Mexico 5-0, Essen, GER
Boris Becker (GER) d. Luis Herrera (MEX) 7-5 6-2 6-3
Marc-Kevin Goellner (GER) d. Alejandro Hernandez (MEX) 7-5 6-3 6-3
Goellner/Jens Knippschild (GER) d. Oscar Ortiz/David Roditi (MEX) 7-6(4) 7-6(4) 4-6 6-3
Boris Becker (GER) d. Alejandro Hernandez (MEX) 6-4 7-5
Jens Knippschild (GER) d. Luis Herrera (MEX) 6-2 3-6 6-4

Russia defeated Romania 3-2, Moscow, RUS
Alexander Volkov (RUS) d. Andrei Pavel (ROM) 6-3 6-7(5) 6-2 6-4
Yevgeny Kafelnikov (RUS) d. Ion Moldovan (ROM) 6-4 7-6(7) 6-4
Andrei Pavel/Gabriel Trifu (ROM) d. Yevgeny Kafelnikov/Andrei Olhovskiy (RUS) 6-4 6-4 6-4
Andrei Pavel (ROM) d. Yevgeny Kafelnikov (RUS) 6-4 3-6 6-4 6-1
Alexander Volkov (RUS) d. Ion Moldovan (ROM) 6-4 6-3 7-5

Slovak Republic defeated Canada 4-1, Montreal, CAN
Karol Kucera (SVK) d. Daniel Nestor (CAN) 6-3 6-3 7-6(0)
Dominik Hrbaty (SVK) d. Sebastien Lareau (CAN) 7-6(7) 4-6 7-6(5) 6-3
Grant Connell/Daniel Nestor (CAN) d. Dominik Hrbaty/Jan Kroslak (SVK) 6-2 6-3 6-4
Karol Kucera (SVK) d. Sebastien Lareau (CAN) 5-7 6-2 6-4 6-3
Dominik Hrbaty (SVK) d. Daniel Nestor (SVK) 6-4 6-7(3) 6-3

Switzerland defeated Korea, Rep 3-2, Locarno, SUI
Marc Rosset (SUI) d. Hyung-Taik Lee (KOR) 6-3 7-6(2) 7-6(4)
Ivo Heuberger (SUI) d. Yong-Il Yoon (KOR) 6-3 6-3 6-4
Lorenzo Manta/Marc Rosset (SUI) d. Hyung-Taik Lee/Yong-Il Yoon (KOR) 7-6(5) 7-6(5) 6-4
Yong-Il Yoon (KOR) d. Lorenzo Manta (SUI) 6-4 6-3
Hyung-Taik Lee (KOR) d. Ivo Heuberger (SUI) 7-5 6-2

Group I

Euro/African Zone

FIRST ROUND
February 7–9

Denmark defeated Hungary 5-0, Aalborg, DEN
Frederik Fetterlein (DEN) d. Jozsef Krocsko (HUN) 6-4 6-2 7-5
Kenneth Carlsen (DEN) d. Attila Savolt (HUN) 6-4 6-4 7-6(3)
Carlsen/Fetterlein (DEN) d. Laszlo Markovits/Attila Savolt (HUN) 7-6(4) 7-6(2) 6-4
Kenneth Carlsen (DEN) d. Jozsef Krocsko (HUN) 6-3 6-7(5) 6-3
Frederik Fetterlein (DEN) d. Attila Savolt (HUN) 5-7 6-3 6-4
Zimbabwe defeated Ukraine 5-0, Harare, ZIM
Wayne Black (ZIM) d. Andrei Medvedev (UKR) 6-4 6-3 4-6 6-4
Bryon Black (ZIM) d. Andrei Rybalko (UKR) 5-7 6-2 7-6(2) 6-3
B. Black/W. Black (ZIM) d. Andrei Medvedev/Dimitri Poliakov (UKR) 6-7(8) 7-5 4-6 6-1 6-4
Byron Black (ZIM) d. Denis Yakimenko (UKR) 6-4 6-4
Wayne Black (ZIM) d. Andrei Rybalko (UKR) 7-6(3) 6-3
Croatia defeated Morocco 4-1, Osijek, CRO
Sasa Hirszon (CRO) d. Karim Alami (MAR) 6-4 6-1 6-3
Goran Ivanisevic (CRO) d. Hicham Arazi (MAR) 6-2 6-2 6-7(4) 6-2
Sasa Hirszon/Goran Ivanisevic (CRO) d. Karim Alami/Hicham Arazi (MAR) 6-2 6-3 6-3
Goran Ivanisevic (CRO) d. Karim Alami (MAR) 6-2 7-5
Hicham Arazi (MAR) d. Sasa Hirszon (CRO) 6-1 6-4

SECOND ROUND
April 4–6

Belgium defeated Denmark 3-2, Brussels, BEL
Filip Dewulf (BEL) d. Kenneth Carlsen (DEN) 6-4 6-0 6-1
Frederik Fetterlein (DEN) d. Johan Van Herck (BEL) 7-6(5) 2-6 6-2 6-1
Kenneth Carlsen/Frederik Fetterlein (DEN) d. Filip Dewulf/Libor Pimek (BEL) 6-3 7-5 1-6 6-4
Johan Van Herck (BEL) d. Kenneth Carlsen (DEN) 6-4 6-1 7-5
Filip Dewulf (BEL) d. Frederik Fetterlein (DEN) 6-0 6-4 3-6 2-6 6-1
Zimbabwe defeated Great Britain 4-1, Crystal Palace, GBR
Wayne Black (ZIM) d. Jamie Delgado (GBR) 2-6 6-3 6-1 6-3
Andrew Richardson (GBR) d. Byron Black (ZIM) 3-6 6-4 1-6 6-4 6-4
Byron Black/Wayne Black (ZIM) d. Neil Broad/Mark Petchey (GBR) 3-6 6-1 6-4 6-7(6) 6-3
Byron Black (ZIM) d. Jamie Delgado (GBR) 6-0 6-0 6-2
Wayne Black (ZIM) d. Andrew Richardson (GBR) 6-3 6-7(5) 7-6(2)
Slovak Republic defeated Israel 3-1, Bratislava, SVK
Dominik Hrbaty (SVK) d. Eyal Ran (ISR) 6-3 4-6 6-3 6-4
Karol Kucera (SVK) d. Noam Behr (ISR) 6-1 6-3 6-0
Noam Behr/Eyal Erlich (ISR) d. Dominik Hrbaty/Karol Kucera (SVK) 6-4 3-6 6-3 7-6(4)
Karol Kucera (SVK) d. Eyal Ran (ISR) 6-2 6-3 6-2
Dominik Hrbaty (SVK) vs Noam Behr (ISR) not played
Austria defeated Croatia 3-2, Graz, AUT
Gilbert Schaller (AUT) d. Goran Ivanisevic (CRO) 6-3 6-4 6-7(3) 2-6 31 ret
Thomas Muster (AUT) d. Sasa Hirszon (CRO) 6-0 6-4 3-6 6-1
Sasa Hirszon/Goran Ivanisevic (CRO) d. Thomas Muster/Udo Plamberger (AUT) 7-5 6-2 6-2
Goran Ivanisevic (CRO) d. Thomas Muster (AUT) 6-7(5) 7-6(5) 6-2 7-5
Gilbert Schaller (AUT) d. Sasa Hirszon (CRO) 6-3 6-3 7-5

SECOND ROUND PLAYOFF
July 11–13

Great Britain defeated Ukraine 3-2, Kiev, UKR
Tim Henman (GBR) d. Andrei Rybalko (UKR) 3-6 6-4 6-3 4-6 6-4
Andrei Medvedev (UKR) d. Greg Rusedski (GBR) 6-1 6-1 2-6 6-2
Henman/Rusedski (GBR) d. Andrei Medvedev/Dimitri Poliakov (UKR) 6-1 6-4 7-6(5)
Andrei Medvedev (UKR) d. Tim Henman (GBR) 6-7(5) 6-3 6-4 6-4
Greg Rusedski (GBR) d. Andrei Rybalko (UKR) 7-5 6-3 6-3

THIRD ROUND PLAYOFF
September 19–21

Ukraine defeated Hungary 3-2, Budapest, HUN
Clay(O): Andrei Medvedev (UKR) d. Kornel Bardoczky (HUN) 6-2 6-2 6-2
Attila Savolt (HUN) d. Andrei Rybalko (UKR) 6-2 6-2 2-6 6-2
Medvedev/Dimitri Poliakov (UKR) d. Gergely Kisgyorgy/Attila Savolt (HUN) 6-2 6-3 6-1
Andrei Medvedev (UKR) d. Attila Savolt (HUN) 6-1 6-7(1) 6-3 5-7 6-2
Kornel Bardoczky (HUN) d. Andrei Rybalko (UKR) 6-0 6-4
Israel defeated Morocco walkover

American Zone

FIRST ROUND
February 7–9

Canada defeated Bahamas 4-1, Montreal, CAN
Daniel Nestor (CAN) d. Roger Smith (BAH) 6-1 6-1 6-2
Mark Knowles (BAH) d. Sebastien Lareau (CAN) 6-4 3-6 6-2 5-7 6-1
Grant Connell/Lareau (CAN) d. Mark Knowles/Roger Smith (BAH) 6-2 6-7(1) 6-4 6-4
Daniel Nestor (CAN) d. Mark Knowles (BAH) 3-6 7-5 6-4 6-2
Sebastien Lareau (CAN) d. Roger Smith (BAH) 6-2 4-6 6-2
Chile defeated Ecuador 4-1, Santiago, CHI
Gabriel Silberstein (CHI) d. Nicolas Lapentti (ECU) 6-2 4-6 1-6 6-3 6-3
Marcelo Rios (CHI) d. Luis Morejon (ECU) 6-1 6-3 3-6 6-2
Pablo Campana/Nicolas Lapentti (ECU) d. Oscar Bustos/Marcelo Rios (CHI) 4-6 6-4 6-0 6-3
Marcelo Rios (CHI) d. Nicolas Lapentti (ECU) 7-5 6-7(6) 6-3 6-7(6) 8-6
Gabriel Silberstein (CHI) d. Luis Morejon (ECU) 7-6(4) 6-2

SECOND ROUND
April 4–6

Canada defeated Venezuela 5-0, Montreal, CAN
Sebastien Lareau (CAN) d. Jose De Armas (VEN) 6-1 6-3 6-2
Daniel Nestor (CAN) d. Jimy Szymanski (VEN) 6-2 7-6(5) 6-1
Grant Connell/Lareau (CAN) d. Shuon Madden/Jimy Szymanski (VEN) 6-2 6-1 6-3
Sebastien Lareau (CAN) d. Jimy Szymanski (VEN) 6-3 7-5
Sebastien Leblanc (CAN) d. Jose De Armas (VEN) 2-6 7-6(2) 6-0
Chile defeated Argentina 3-2, Santiago, CHI
Marcelo Rios (CHI) d. Javier Frana (ARG) 6-1 6-4 7-6(2)
Hernan Gumy (ARG) d. Gabriel Silberstein (CHI) 6-0 6-4 6-4
Rios/Silberstein (CHI) d. Javier Frana/Luis Lobo (ARG) 3-6 7-6(8) 4-6 6-3 6-2
Marcelo Rios (CHI) d. Hernan Gumy (ARG) 6-4 7-5 6-4
Javier Frana (ARG) d. Gabriel Silberstein (CHI) 6-4 6-4

SECOND ROUND PLAYOFF
July 11–13

Bahamas defeated Venezuela 3-2, Nassau, BAH
Roger Smith (BAH) d. Nicolas Pereira (VEN) 7-6(4) 6-3 6-4
Jimy Szymanski (VEN) d. Mark Knowles (BAH) 6-3 7-6(4) 6-2
Knowles/Smith (BAH) d. Nicolas Pereira/Jimy Szymanski (VEN) 6-3 6-7(4) 7-6(5) 7-5
Nicolas Pereira (VEN) d. Mark Knowles (BAH) 5-7 7-5 6-1 7-5
Roger Smith (BAH) d. Jimy Szymanski (VEN) 3-6 1-6 7-6(4) 6-4 6-4
Ecuador defeated Argentina 3-1, Buenos Aires, ARG
Luis Morejon (ECU) d. Hernan Gumy (ARG) 6-1 6-4 5-7 7-5
Nicolas Lapentti (ECU) d. Marcelo Charpentier (ARG) 6-3 6-4 6-3
Pablo Albano/Luis Lobo (ARG) d. Giorgio Carneade/Nicolas Lapentti (ECU) 6-2 6-1 7-6(4)
Nicolas Lapentti (ECU) d. Hernan Gumy (ARG) 6-4 6-4 3-6 0-6 6-3
Luis Morejon (ECU) v Marcelo Charpentier (ARG) not played - rain

THIRD ROUND PLAYOFF
September 19–21

Argentina defeated Venezuela 4-1, Buenos Aires, ARG
Hernan Gumy (ARG) d. Jose De Armas (VEN) 6-0 6-2 6-1
Lucas Arnold (ARG) d. Jimy Szymanski (VEN) 6-4 6-3 7-5
Pablo Albano/Luis Lobo (ARG) d. Jose De Armas/Jimy Szymanski (VEN) 6-1 6-0 6-3
Jimy Szymanski (VEN) d. Luis Lobo (ARG) 6-2 6-2
Lucas Arnold (ARG) d. Jose De Armas (VEN) 6-1 6-2

Asia/Oceania Zone

FIRST ROUND
February 4–6

China defeated Uzbekistan 4-1, Beijing, CHN
Jia-Ping Xia (CHN) d. Dmitri Tomashevich (UZB) 6-4 7-6(5) 6-3
Oleg Ogorodov (UZB) d. Bing Pan (CHN) 6-2 6-4 7-5
Bing Pan/Jia-Ping Xia (CHN) d. Oleg Ogorodov/Dmitri Tomashevich (UZB) 7-6(4) 6-3 2-6 6-2
Jia-Ping Xia (CHN) d. Oleg Ogorodov (UZB) 6-4 4-6 7-6(5) 7-6(7)
Bing Pan (CHN) d. Dmitri Tomashevich (UZB) 6-4 7-6(3)
Korea defeated Japan 3-2, Seoul, KOR
Yong-Il Yoon (KOR) d. Takao Suzuki (JPN) 1-6 7-5 6-3 6-1
Shuzo Matsuoka (JPN) d. Hyung-Taik Lee (KOR) 7-6(5) 6-3 7-6(3)
Satoshi Iwabuchi/Suzuki (JPN) d. Hyung-Taik Lee/Yong-Il Yoon (KOR) 6-3 6-4 3-6 4-6 8-6
Yong-Il Yoon (KOR) d. Shuzo Matsuoka (JPN) 6-2 6-4 6-3
Hyung-Taik Lee (KOR) d. Takao Suzuki (JPN) 3-6 6-4 1-6 6-4 6-4 (Played 7-9 February)

Indonesia defeated Philippines 3-2, Manila, PHI
Robert Angelo (PHI) d. Suwandi Suwandi (INA) 7-6(8) 7-6(5) 6-3
Joseph Lizardo (PHI) d. Andrian Raturandang (INA) 6-4 5-7 7-5 6-2
Sulistyo Wibowo/ Bonit Wiryawan (INA) d. Michael Misa/Pio Tolentino (PHI) 6-1 6-4 6-0
Suwandi Suwandi (INA) d. Joseph Lizardo (PHI) 6-2 1-6 6-3 5-7 6-2
Bonit Wiryawan (INA) d. Robert Angelo (PHI) 6-3 1-6 4-6 6-1 6-3

SECOND ROUND
April 4–6

New Zealand defeated Indonesia 5-0, Jakarta, INA
Mark Nielsen (NZL) d. Suwandi Suwandi (INA) 7-5 6-3 6-4
Alistair Hunt (NZL) d. Andrian Raturandang (INA) 6-3 6-0 6-3
James Greenhalgh/Hunt (NZL) d. Sulistyo Wibowo/Bonit Wiryawan (INA) 6-3 6-4 3-6 6-3
Glenn Wilson (NZL) d. Suwandi Suwandi (INA) 6-4 7-5
Mark Nielsen (NZL) d. Andrian Raturandang (INA) 6-2 7-5
Korea defeated China 4-1, Beijing, CHN
Hyung-Taik Lee (KOR) d. Jia-Ping Xia (CHN) 6-1 2-6 2-6 7-6(3) 6-1
Yong-Il Yoon (KOR) d. Bing Pan (CHN) 6-3 6-4 6-2
Hyung-Taik Lee/Yong-Il Yoon (KOR) d. Bing Pan/Jia-Ping Xia (CHN) 6-4 3-6 6-2 6-4
Yong-Il Yoon (KOR) d. Yu Zheng (CHN) 6-3 7-5
Bing Pan (CHN) d. Dong-Hyun Kim (KOR) 7-6(5) 6-4

SECOND ROUND PLAYOFF
July 11–13

Japan defeated Uzbekistan 3-2, Tashkent, UZB
Oleg Ogorodov (UZB) d. Hideki Kaneko (JPN) 6-1 7-5 4-6 6-3
Gouichi Motomura (JPN) d. Dmitri Tomashevich (UZB) 6-1 2-6 6-1 6-3
Satoshi Iwabuchi/Takao Suzuki (JPN) d. Vadim Kutsenko/Oleg Ogorodov (UZB) 6-3 6-4 6-2
Oleg Ogorodov (UZB) d. Gouichi Motomura (JPN) 6-2 6-2 6-2
Hideki Kaneko (JPN) d. Dmitri Tomashevich (UZB) 6-3 4-6 6-1 6-4

THIRD ROUND PLAYOFF
September 19–21

Uzbekistan defeated Philippines 5-0, Tashkent, UZB
Oleg Ogorodov (UZB) d. Michael Misa (PHI) 6-3 6-3 6-0
Dmitri Tomashevich (UZB) d. Joseph Lizardo (PHI) 4-6 6-2 6-2 7-5
Ogorodov/Tomashevich (UZB) d. Robert Angelo/Joseph Lizardo (PHI) 6-2 6-1 6-3
Oleg Ogorodov (UZB) d. Joseph Lizardo (PHI) 6-3 6-4
Dmitri Tomashevich (UZB) d. Michael Misa (PHI) 6-1 6-1

Group II

American Zone

FIRST ROUND
February 7–9

Peru defeated Cuba 3-2, Havana, CUB
Lazaro Navarro (CUB) d. Alejandro Aramburu (PER) 6-1 6-4 6-2
Americo Venero (PER) d. Juan Pino (CUB) 6-4 7-5 5-7 6-3
Americo Venero/Jaime Yzaga (PER) d. Lazaro Navarro/Juan Pino (CUB) 6-4 6-4 6-2
Juan Pino (CUB) d. Jaime Yzaga (PER) 4-6 7-6(4) 10 (defaulted)
Americo Venero (PER) d. Lazaro Navarro (CUB) 7-6(5) 6-3 6-7(5) 2-6 8-6
Colombia defeated Puerto Rico 3-2, San Juan, PUR
Jorge Gonzalez (PUR) d. Miguel Tobon (COL) 6-2 6-2 4-6 6-4
Mauricio Hadad (COL) d. Rafael Jordan (PUR) 6-4 6-0 5-7 6-2
Hadad/Tobon (COL) d. Ernesto Fernandez/Jorge Gonzalez (PUR) 7-6(5) 6-3 6-4
Mauricio Hadad (COL) d. Jorge Gonzalez (PUR) 6-3 6-2 6-3
Rafael Jordan (PUR) d. Miguel Tobon (COL) 6-3 7-6(7)
Paraguay defeated Haiti 5-0, Asuncion, PAR
Ricardo Mena (PAR) d. Ronald Agenor (HAI) 6-4 6-0 6-2
Ramon Delgado (PAR) d. Bertrand Madsen (HAI) 7-5 6-3 6-1
Delgado/Mena (PAR) d. Agenor/Madsen (HAI) 6-4 4-6 7-5
Ramon Delgado (PAR) d. Bertrand Lacombe (HAI) 6-1 6-3
Ricardo Mena (PAR) d. Bertrand Madsen (HAI) 6-2 6-4
Uruguay defeated El Salvador 4-1, San Salvador, ESA
Federico Dondo (URU) d. Manuel Tejada (ESA) 6-4 6-0
Marcelo Filippini (URU) d. Jose Baires (ESA) 6-0 7-5 6-3
Dondo/Gonzalo Rodriguez (URU) d. Jorge Mendez/Tejada (ESA) 6-3 7-6(4) 6-2
Manuel Tejada (ESA) d. Marcelo Filippini (URU) 31 ret
Federico Dondo (URU) d. Jose Baires (ESA) 6-3 6-2

SECOND ROUND
April 4–6

Colombia defeated Peru 5-0, Cali, COL
Jaime Cortes (COL) d. Alejandro Aramburu (PER) 6-3 7-5 7-5
Miguel Tobon (COL) d. Luis Horna (PER) 6-7(4) 6-4 6-2 6-2
Mario Rincon/Miguel Tobon (COL) d. Cesar Reano/Jaime Yzaga (PER) 7-5 6-3 7-6(3)
Miguel Tobon (COL) d. Alejandro Aramburu (PER) 6-4 7-6(3)
Eduardo Rincon (COL) d. Luis Horna (PER) 4-6 6-4 7-6(6)
Uruguay defeated Paraguay 3-2, Asuncion, PAR
Ramon Delgado (PAR) d. Federico Dondo (URU) 3-6 6-2 6-2 7-5
Marcelo Filippini (URU) d. Ricardo Mena (PAR) 6-4 6-4 6-4
Filippini/Gonzalo Rodriguez (URU) d. Delgado/Mena (PAR) 3-6 6-3 6-1 6-2
Marcelo Filippini (URU) d. Ramon Delgado (PAR) 7-5 4-6 7-6(6) 6-2
Ricardo Mena (PAR) d. Federico Dondo (URU) 6-3 7-5

THIRD ROUND
September 19–21

Colombia defeated Uruguay 4-1, Bogota, COL
Mario Rincon (COL) d. Federico Dondo (URU) 5-7 7-6(5) 6-3 6-0
Miguel Tobon (COL) d. Marcelo Filippini (URU) 7-6(3) 5-7 7-6(5) 6-1
Rincon/Tobon (COL) d. Filippini/Gonzalo Rodriguez (URU) 6-2 6-3 6-7(1) 7-5
Marcelo Filippini (URU) d. Mario Rincon (COL) 6-2 6-2
Philippe Moggio (COL) d. Federico Dondo (URU) 6-3 6-4

PLAYOFF TIES
April 4–6

Cuba defeated Puerto Rico 4-1, San Juan, PUR
Juan Pino (CUB) d. Hector Nevares (PUR) 6-1 6-4
Lazarro Navarro (CUB) d. Rafael Jordan (PUR) 6-4 5-7 6-1 3-6 6-1
Navarro/Pino (CUB) d. Ernie Fernandez/Jordan (PUR) 3-6 6-4 3-6 6-4 6-4
Ernie Fernandez (PUR) d. Jorge Cordova (CUB) 2-6 6-4 6-2
Lazarro Navarro (CUB) d. Hector Nevares (PUR) 6-4 6-0
Haiti defeated El Salvador 3-2, San Salvador, ESA
Bertrand Madsen (HAI) d. Jose Baires (ESA) 7-5 6-3 6-1
Manuel Tejada (ESA) d. Bertrand Lacombe (HAI) 7-6(4) 6-3 6-4
Lacombe/Madsen (HAI) d. Jorge Mendez/Tejada (ESA) 6-2 6-4 7-6(6)
Bertrand Madsen (HAI) d. Manuel Tejada (ESA) 6-2 7-6(4) 6-3
Jose Baires (ESA) d. Raphael Goscinny (HAI) 6-2 6-4

Asia/Oceania Zone

FIRST ROUND
February 14–16

Thailand defeated Hong Kong 5-0, Hong Kong, HKG
Woraphol Thongkhamchu (THA) d. Mark Ferreira (HKG) 6-3 6-2 6-0
Wittaya Samrej (THA) d. Melvin Tong (HKG) 6-3 5-7 6-2 2-6 6-4
Narathorn and Thanakorn Srichaphan (THA) d. Ferreira/Graeme Foster (HKG) 6-1 6-2 6-3
Wittaya Samrej (THA) d. Mark Ferreira (HKG) 6-2 6-2
Woraphol Thongkhamchu (THA) d. Wayne Wong (HKG) 6-3 7-6(2)

February 18–20

Lebanon defeated Saudi Arabia 5-0, Riyadh, KSA
Ali Hamadeh (LIB) d. Othman Al-Anazi (KSA) 6-1 6-2 6-4
Sean Karam (LIB) d. Bader Al-Megayal (KSA) 6-4 6-3 6-4
Ali Hamadeh/Sean Karam (LIB) d. Othman Al-Anazi/Bader Al-Megayal (KSA) 6-4 6-1 6-3
Ali Hamadeh (LIB) d. Bader Al-Megayal (KSA) 6-0 6-1
Toufiq Zahlan (LIB) d. Moafa Tawfiq (KSA) 7-5 6-3

February 21–23

Chinese Taipei defeated Singapore 5-0, Taipei, TPE
Yu-Hui Lien (TPE) d. Chee-Yen Chen (SIN) 6-2 6-0 6-0
Chia-Yen Tsai (TPE) d. Kuen-Yiep Ho (SIN) 6-2 6-1 6-0
Jinn-Yen Chiang/ Yu-Hui Lien (TPE) d. Kuen-Yiep Ho/ Yung-Yi Kho (SIN) 6-2 6-3 6-2
Chia-Yen Tsai (TPE) d. Chee-Yen Chen (SIN) 6-2 6-2
Yu-Hui Lien (TPE) d. Ee-Wei Tan (SIN) 6-1 6-0
Iran defeated Pakistan 3-2, Islamabad ,PAK
Mansour Bahrami (IRI) d. Omer Rashid (PAK) 6-3 6-4 0-6 6-4
Hameed Ul-Haq (PAK) d. Mohammad-Reza Tavakoli (IRI) 7-6(2) 3-6 6-2 6-4
Mansour Bahrami/Ramin Raziani (IRI) d. Omer Rashid/Asim Shafik (PAK) 6-3 7-5 7-6(3)
Ramin Raziani (IRI) d. Omer Rashid (PAK) 4-6 6-3 6-2 6-4
Hameed Ul-Haq (PAK) d. Mansour Bahrami (IRI) 1-6 6-4 6-2

SECOND ROUND
April 4–6

Iran defeated Chinese Taipei 4-1, Tehran, IRI
Ramin Raziani (IRI) d. Yu-Hui Lien (TPE) 4-6 2-6 7-6(5) 6-4 6-3
Mansour Bahrami (IRI) d. Chih-Jung Chen (TPE) 7-5 7-6(3) 3-6 6-3 Mansour Bahrami/Ramin Raziani (IRI) d. Chih-Jung Chen/Yu-Hui Lien (TPE) 6-4 7-6(6) 7-6(4)
Chih-Jung Chen (TPE) d. Ramin Raziani (IRI) 20 ret
Mansour Bahrami (IRI) d. Chia-Yen Tsai (TPE) 6-0 7-6(2)

Lebanon defeated Thailand 5-0, Beirut, LIB
Hisham Zaatini (LIB) d. Wittaya Samrej (THA) 3-6 6-3 6-3 6-2
Ali Hamadeh (LIB) d. Narathorn Srichaphan (THA) 7-6(5) 7-5 7-6(4)
Hamadeh/Zaatini (LIB) d. Narathorn and Thanakorn Srichaphan (THA) 6-4 3-6 7-6(2) 6-4
Ali Hamadeh (LIB) d. Wittaya Samrej (THA) 6-3 3-6 7-6(5)
Hisham Zaatini (LIB) d. Thanakorn Srichaphan (THA) 6-4 6-1

THIRD ROUND
September 19–21

Lebanon defeated Iran 4-1, Zouk Mikail, LIB
Ali Hamadeh (LIB) d. Reza Nakhai (IRI) 6-3 7-5 6-4
Hicham Zaatini (LIB) d. Mohammad-Reza Tavakoli (IRI) 6-2 6-1 6-3
Ali Hamadeh/Hicham Zaatini (LIB) d. Reza Nakhai/Seyed-Akhar Taheri (IRI) 6-4 6-4 6-3
Hicham Zaatini (LIB) d. Reza Nakhai (IRI) 7-6(3) 6-3
Mohammad-Reza Tavakoli (IRI) d. Toufik Zahlan (LIB) 6-2 6-4

PLAYOFF TIES
April 4–6

Pakistan defeated Singapore 5-0, Islamabad, PAK
Omer Rashid (PAK) d. Kuen-Yip Ho (SIN) 6-3 6-0 7-5
Hameed Ul-Haq (PAK) d. Sherman Lim (SIN) 6-4 6-2 6-1
Omer Rashid/Hameed Ul-Haq (PAK) d. Kuen-Yip Ho/Sherman Lim (SIN) 6-3 6-3 6-2
Asim Shafik (PAK) d. Sherman Lim (SIN) 6-1 6-4
Nasir Sherazi (PAK) d. Jensen Hiu (SIN) 6-1 6-3

Hong Kong defeated Saudi Arabia 4-1, Riyadh, KSA
Bader Al-Megayel (KSA) d. Wayne Wong (HKG) 6-4 7-6(5) 6-3
Melvin Tong (HKG) d. Farah Somali (KSA) 6-2 6-0 6-0
Mark Ferreira/Melvin Tong (HKG) d. Tawfiq Al-Ibrahim/Bader Al-Megayel (KSA) 6-0 6-1 6-4
Melvin Tong (HKG) d. Bader Al-Megayel (KSA) 7-5 6-2 6-3
Wayne Wong (HKG) d. Moafa Tawfiq (KSA) 6-2 6-3

Euro/African Zone

FIRST ROUND
May 2–4

Norway defeated Nigeria 5-0, Snaroya, NOR
Jan Frode Andersen (NOR) d. Sule Ladipo (NGR) 6-1 6-0 6-4
Christian Ruud (NOR) d. Ganiyu Adelekan (NGR) 6-0 6-1 6-0
Helge Koll/Christian Ruud (NOR) d. Ganiyu Adelekan/Sule Ladipo (NGR) 6-2 4-6 6-1 7-6(5)
Christian Ruud (NOR) d. Dickson Ogu (NGR) 6-0 6-0
Thomas Heyerdahl (NOR) d. Ganiyu Adelekan (NGR) 7-5 6-3

Slovenia defeated Georgia 3-2, Tbilisi, GEO
Iztok Bozic (SLO) d. Vladimir Margalitadze (GEO) 6-2 6-3 6-1
Vladimir Gabrichidze (GEO) d. Borut Urh (SLO) 6-3 7-5 1-6 3-6 6-4
Marko Por/Urh (SLO) d. VGabrichidze /David Katcharava (GEO) 7-6(6) 7-5 6-7(2) 6-2
Borut Urh (SLO) d. Vladimir Margalitadze (GEO) 6-2 6-2 6-0
Vladimir Gabrichidze (GEO) d. Andrei Krasevec (SLO) 4-6 7-6(2) 6-2

Portugal defeated Egypt 5-0, Cairo, EGY
Nuno Marques (POR) d. Gehad El Deeb (EGY) 6-0 6-4 7-6(5)
Emanuel Couto (POR) d. Amr Ghoneim (EGY) 2-6 6-4 7-5 6-3
Emanuel Couto/Bernardo Mota (POR) d. Adli El Shafei/ Amr Ghoneim (EGY) 7-5 6-1 6-0
Joao Cunha-Silva (POR) d. Amr Ghoneim (EGY) 6-4 6-3
Emanuel Couto (POR) d. Gehad El Deeb (EGY) 6-4 7-5

Yugoslavia defeated Lithuania 3-2, Vilnius, LTU
Nenad Zimonjic (YUG) d. Rolandos Murashka (LTU) 6-3 6-1 6-3
Bojan Vujic (YUG) d. Eugenius Cariovas (LTU) 7-6(3) 7-6(4) 6-2
Dusan Vemic/Zimonjic (YUG) d. Cariovas/Murashka (LTU) 6-4 6-4 6-4
Rolandos Murashka (LTU) d. Bojan Vujic (YUG) 7-5 6-4
Eugenius Cariovas (LTU) d. Vladimir Pavicevic (YUG) 7-6(5) 4-6 6-3

Cote D'Ivoire defeated Latvia 5-0, Abidjan, CIV
Claude N'Goran (LTU) d. Ivo Lagzdins (LAT) 6-1 6-2 6-0
Clement N'Goran (LTU) d. Raimonds Sproga (LAT) 6-4 6-0 6-2
Claude N'Goran/Clement N'Goran (LTU) d. Ivo Lagzdins/Raimonds Sproga (LAT) 6-1 6-2 7-5
Ilou Lonfo (LTU) d. Raimonds Sproga (LAT) 6-1 6-2
Valentin Sanon (LTU) d. Oskars Vaskis (LAT) 6-4 6-4

Poland defeated Ghana 5-0, Poznan, POL
Bartlomiej Dabrowski (POL) d. Daniel Omaboe (GHA) 6-0 6-2 6-2
Filip Aniola (POL) d. Frank Ofori (GHA) 6-1 6-3 6-0
Dabrowski/Bernard Kaczorowski (POL) d. Nortey Dowuona/Ofori (GHA) 6-1 6-2 7-6(5)
Krystian Pfeiffer (POL) d. Nortey Dowuona (GHA) 6-1 6-1
Filip Aniola (POL) d. Alex Ofori (GHA) 6-1 6-0

Belarus defeated Ireland 4-1, Dublin, IRL
Maxim Mirnyi (BLR) d. Scott Barron (IRL) 6-2 6-3 4-6 6-4
Owen Casey (IRL) d. Alexander Shvec (BLR) 6-2 4-6 6-3 4-6 7-5
Maxim Mirnyi/Vladimir Voltchkov (BLR) d. Scott Barron/Tom Hamilton (IRL) 6-4 7-6(5) 6-3
Alexander Shvec (BLR) d. Scott Barron (IRL) 6-1 6-2 7-6(4)
Maxim Mirnyi (BLR) d. Eoin Collins (IRL) 7-5 6-3

Finland defeated Greece 3-2, Helsinki, FIN
Anastassios Vasiliadis (GRE) d. Tuomas Ketola (FIN) 6-2 1-6 6-7(6) 6-4 6-4
Konstantinos Economidis (GRE) d. Kim Tiilikainen (FIN) 6-7(4) 7-5 6-4 6-1
Ketola/Ville Liukko (FIN) d. Economidis/Vasiliadis (GRE) 6-3 7-6(8) 6-4
Ville Liukko (FIN) d. Konstantinos Economidis (GRE) 6-3 6-4 6-4
Kim Tiilikainen (FIN) d. Anastassios Vasiliadis (GRE) 6-3 7-6(3) 7-6(3)

SECOND ROUND
July 11–13

Norway defeated Slovenia 4-1, Nova Gorica, SLO
Christian Ruud (NOR) d. Iztok Bozic (SLO) 4-6 6-2 6-4 6-3
Jan-Frode Andersen (NOR) d. Blaz Trupej (SLO) 4-6 6-4 6-3 6-1
Andrej Karsevec/Marco Por (SLO) d. Helge Koll/Christian Ruud (NOR) 6-2 6-3 5-7 1-6 6-2
Jan-Frode Andersen (NOR) d. Iztok Bozic (SLO) 6-3 1-6 6-3 6-2
Christian Ruud (NOR) d. Blaz Trupej (SLO) 6-4 6-4

Portugal defeated Yugoslavia 3-2, Porto, POR
Joao Cunha-Silva (POR) d. Nenad Zimonjic (YUG) 2-6 6-4 6-4 6-4
Bojan Vujic (YUG) d. Emanuel Couto (POR) 6-3 7-5 5-7 6-2
Couto/Bernardo Mota (POR) d. Nebojsa Djordjevic/Zimonjic (YUG) 6-4 6-4 6-4
Bojan Vujic (YUG) d. Joao Cunha-Silva (POR) 6-4 6-3 3-6 4-6 6-3
Emanuel Couto (POR) d. Nenad Zimonjic (YUG) 6-7(2) 7-5 7-5 6-3

Poland defeated Cote d'Ivoire 4-1, Bytom, POL
Claude N'Goran (LTU) d. Michal Chmela (POL) 6-4 5-7 6-2 6-7(4) 6-4
Bartlomiej Dabrowski (POL) d. Jean-Christophe Nabi (LTU) 7-6(1) 6-1 6-4
Dabrowski/Michal Gawlowski (POL) d. Ilou Lonfo/N'Goran (LTU) 6-4 7-6(7) 3-6 6-2
Bartlomiej Dabrowski (POL) d. Claude N'Goran (LTU) 6-4 6-1 6-0
Michal Chmela (POL) d. Nouhoun Sangare (LTU) 6-1 6-2

Finland defeated Belarus 3-2, Tampere, FIN
Vladimir Voltchkov (BLR) d. Tuomas Ketola (FIN) 6-3 3-6 7-6(5) 6-1
Tommi Lenho (FIN) d. Alexander Shvec (BLR) 7-5 6-1 4-6 4-6 6-3
Ketola/Ville Liukko (FIN) d. Shvec/Voltchkov (BLR) 3-6 6-4 6-1 6-1
Kim Tiilikainen (FIN) d. Alexander Shvec (BLR) 6-7(6) 6-1 7-5 6-7(6) 6-0
Vladimir Voltchkov (BLR) d. Ville Liukko (FIN) 6-1 4-6 7-5

THIRD ROUND
September 19–21

Norway defeated Portugal 3-2, Oporto, POR
Jan-Frode Andersen (NOR) d. Nuno Marques (POR) 7-5 6-1 1-6 6-3
Christian Ruud (NOR) d. Emanuel Couto (POR) 6-1 6-1 6-1
Emanuel Couto/Bernado Mota (POR) d. Helge Koll/Christian Ruud (NOR) 6-4 7-6(1) 4-6 6-2
Christian Ruud (NOR) d. Nuno Marques (POR) 7-6(1) 7-6(5) 7-6(2)
Bernado Mota (POR) d. Helge Koll (NOR) 6-2 6-3

Finland defeated Poland 3-2, Helsinki, FIN
Bartlomiej Dabrowski (POL) d. Ville Liukko (FIN) 4-6 7-5 7-5 6-1
Michal Chmela (POL) d. Tuomas Ketola (FIN) 3-6 6-2 2-6 6-4 6-4
Ketola/Ville Liukko (FIN) d. Chmela/Dabrowski (POL) 7-6(4) 6-7(9) 6-0 4-6 6-3
Tuomas Ketola (FIN) d. Bartlomiej Dabrowski (POL) 7-6(4) 6-1 7-6(4)
Ville Luikko (FIN) d. Michal Chmela (POL) 3-6 3-6 6-4 6-3 6-4

PLAYOFF ROUND
July 11–13

Georgia defeated Nigeria 5-0, Tbilisi, GEO
David Katcharava (GEO) d. Ganiyu Adelekan (NGR) 6-1 6-2 6-1
Vladimir Gabrichidze (GEO) d. Sule Ladipo (NGR) 6-3 6-2 6-3
Gabrichidze/Katcharava (GEO) d. Adelekan/Ladipo (NGR) 6-7(8) 6-3 6-2 7-5
Givi Samkaradze (GEO) d. Sule Ladipo (NGR) 6-3 ret
Vladimir Gabrichidze (GEO) d. Ganiyu Adelekan (NGR) 6-1 6-2

Egypt defeated Lithuania 3-2, Cairo, EGY
Rolandas Murashka (LTU) d. Gehad El Deeb (EGY) 4-6 6-4 6-2 6-0
Amr Ghoneim (EGY) d. Eugenius Cariovas (LTU) 3-6 6-2 7-6(5) 6-4
Ghoneim/Hisham Hemeda (EGY) d. Cariovas/Murashka (LTU) 7-6(1) 7-6(4) 4-6 7-6(4)
Rolandas Murashka (LTU) d. Amr Ghoneim (EGY) 6-1 3-6 4-6 6-3 6-3
Hisham Hemeda (EGY) d. Eugenious Cariovas (LTU) 6-2 7-6(4) 6-7(5) 5-7 119

Latvia defeated Ghana 4-1, Jurmala, LAT
Girts Dzelde (LAT) d. Gunther Darkey (GHA) 6-2 6-1 6-1
Andris Filimonovs (LAT) d. Frank Ofori (GHA) 6-1 6-2 6-2
Girts Dzelde/Andris Filimonovs (LAT) d. Frank Ofori/Tetteh Quaye (GHA) 6-1 6-1 6-0
Frank Ofori (GHA) d. Girts Dzelde (LAT) 7-6(5) 6-4
Andris Filimonovs (LAT) d. Gunther Darkey (GHA) 6-3 6-2
Ireland defeated Greece 4-1, Dublin, IRL
Owen Casey (IRL) d. Solon Peppas (GRE) 6-1 6-1 6-0
Konstantinos Economidis (GRE) d. Scott Barron (IRL) 2-6 2-6 6-3 6-2 6-4
Scott Barron/Owen Casey (IRL) d. Konstantinos Economidis/Nikos Rovas (GRE) 6-2 6-3 6-2
Scott Barron (IRL) d. Solon Peppas (GRE) 6-3 6-0 6-1
Owen Casey (IRL) d. Konstantinos Economidis (GRE) 6-1 6-4

Group III

Euro/African Zone A
January 22-26, Dakar, Senegal

Group A: Ethiopia, FYR Macedonia, San Marino, Turkey
Group B: Armenia, Bosnia/Herzegovina, Luxembourg, Senegal

GROUP A

January 22

FYR of Macedonia defeated San Marino 3-0
Dragan Jovanovski (MKD) d. Cristian Rosti (SMR) 6-1 2-6 6-3
Zoran Sevcenko (MKD) d. Domenico Vicini (SMR) 6-1 6-3
Lazar Magdincev/Zoran Sevcenko (MKD) d. Gabriel Francini/Domenico Vicini (SMR) 6-1 7-6(5)
Turkey defeated Ethiopia 3-0
Baris Ergun (TUR) d. Habtamu Kidan (ETH) 6-0 6-7(5) 6-3
Erhan Oral (TUR) d. Yohannes Setegne (ETH) 6-2 6-3
Mustafa Azkara/Alaaddin Karagoz (TUR) d. Samuel Gabriel/Yohannes Setegne (ETH) 6-0 6-3

January 23

Turkey defeated San Marino 3-0
Baris Ergun (TUR) d. Cristian Rosti (SMR) 6-4 6-2
Erhan Oral (TUR) d. Domenico Vicini (SMR) 6-1 6-4
Mustafa Azkara/Alaaddin Karagoz (TUR) d. Gabriel Francini/Domenico Vicini (SMR) 6-3 6-3
FYR of Macedonia defeated Ethiopia 2-1
Samuel Gabriel (ETH) d. Dragan Jovanovski (MKD) 2-6 6-4 6-0
Zoran Sevcenko (MKD) d. Yohannes Setegne (ETH) 6-0 6-0
Lazar Magdincev/Zoran Sevcenko (MKD) d. Samuel Gabriel/Habtamu Kidan (ETH) 6-2 6-1

January 24

FYR of Macedonia defeated Turkey 2-1
Alaaddin Karagoz (TUR) d. Lazar Magdincev (MKD) 6-4 6-4
Zoran Sevcenko (MKD) d. Baris Ergun (TUR) 6-4 6-0
Lazar Magdincev/Zoran Sevcenko (MKD) d. Mustafa Azkara/ Erhan Oral (TUR) 7-5 6-2
San Marino defeated Ethiopia 2-1
Cristian Rosti (SMR) d. Habtamu Kidan (ETH) 6-4 6-1
Domenico Vicini (SMR) d. Samuel Gabriel (ETH) 6-2 6-4
Kidan/Yohannes Setegne (ETH) d. Gabriel Francini/Massiliano Rosti (SMR) 6-3 7-6(4)

GROUP B

January 22

Senegal defeated Armenia 3-0
Jean Noel Said (SEN) d. Artak Aroutiounyan (ARM) 6-3 6-4
Yahiya Doumbia (SEN) d. David Babayan (ARM) 6-0 6-0
Yahiya Doumbia/Thierno Ly (SEN) d. Haik Hakobyan/Artak Aroutiounyan (ARM) 6-2 6-3.
Luxembourg defeated Bosnia/Herzegovina 2-1
Johnny Goudenbour (LUX) d. Eldar Mustafic (BIH) 6-3 6-3
Merid Zahirovic (BIH) d. Sacha Thoma (LUX) 7-6(11) 6-1
Johnny Goudenbour/Pascal Schaul (LUX) d. Eldar Mustafic/Merid Zahirovic (BIH) 4-6 6-3 6-4

January 23

Senegal defeated Bosnia/Herzegovina 3-0
Jean Noel Said (SEN) d. Haris Basalic (BIH) 7-6(4) 6-3
Yahiya Doumbia (SEN) d. Merid Zahirovic (BIH) 6-1 6-2
Yahiya Doumbia/Thierno Ly (SEN) d. Haris Basalic/Eldar Mustafic (BIH) 6-3 6-4

Luxembourg defeated Armenia 3-0
Adrian Graimprey (LUX) d. Artak Aroutiounyan (ARM) 6-0 6-0
Sacha Thoma (LUX) d. David Babayan (ARM) 6-1 6-1
Johnny Goudenbour/Pascal Schaul (LUX) d. Aroutiounyan/Anri Makichyan (ARM) 6-2 6-3

January 24

Senegal defeated Luxembourg 2-1
Pascal Schaul (LUX) d. Jean Noel Said (SEN) 6-4 6-4
Yahiya Doumbia (SEN) d. Adrian Graimprey (LUX) 5-7 6-4 6-2
Yahiya Doumbia/Thierno Ly (SEN) d. Johnny Goudenbour/Sacha Thoma (LUX) 7-6(7) 6-2
Bosnia/Herzegovina defeated Armenia 3-0
Eldar Mustafic (BIH) d. Artak Aroutiounyan (ARM) 6-3 6-3
Merid Zahirovic (BIH) d. David Babayan (ARM) 6-2 6-1
Eldar Mustafic/Merid Zahirovic (BIH) d. Haik Hakobyan/Anri Makichyan (ARM) 6-4 6-2

SEMIFINALS

Luxembourg defeated FYR of Macedonia 2-1
Johnny Goudenbour (LUX) d. Lazar Magdincev (MKD) 6-2 6-3
Zoran Sevcenko (MKD) d. Sacha Thoma (LUX) 6-1 6-4
Goudenbour/Adrian Graimprey (LUX) d.Magdincev/Sevcenko (MKD) 7-6(3) 6-7(3) 6-2
Senegal defeated Turkey 2-1
Baris Ergun (TUR) d. Jean Noel Said (SEN) 4-6 6-3 6-3
Yahiya Doumbia (SEN) d. Erhan Oral (TUR) 6-2 6-3
Yahiya Doumbia/Thierno Ly (SEN) d. Baris Ergun/Alaaddin Karagoz (TUR) 6-4 6-4

FINAL

Luxembourg defeated Senegal 2-1
Pascal Schaul (LUX) d. Jean Noel Said (SEN) 6-2 6-4
Yahiya Doumbia (SEN) d. Sacha Thoma (LUX) 6-2 6-2
Johnny Goudenbour/Adrian Graimprey (LUX) d. Doumbia/Thierno Ly (SEN) 7-6(4) 7-6(5)

PLAYOFF FOR 3RD/4TH POSITIONS

Turkey defeated FYR of Macedonia 2-1
Mustafa Azkara (TUR) d. Goran Popov (MKD) 6-4 6-1
Zoran Sevcenko (MKD) d. Baris Ergun (TUR) 6-7(4) 6-2 8-6
Mustafa Azkara/Erhan Oral (TUR) d. Lazar Magdincev/Zoran Sevcenko (MKD) 6-4 6-2

PLAYOFFS FOR 5TH – 8TH POSITIONS

San Marino defeated Armenia 3-0
Cristian Rosti (SMR) d. Anri Makichyan (ARM) 6-1 6-2
Domenico Vicini (SMR) d. Artak Aroutiounyan (ARM) 5-7 7-5 6-3
Gabriel Francini/Cristian Rosti (SMR) d. Haik Hakobyan/Anri Makichyan (ARM) 6-4 6-2
Bosnia/Herzegovina defeated Ethiopia 3-0
Eldar Mustafic (BIH) d. Samuel Gabriel (ETH) 6-1 6-2
Merid Zahirovic (BIH) d. Yohannes Setegne (ETH) 2-6 6-3 6-1
Haris Basalic/Eldar Mustafic (BIH) d. Habtamu Kidan/Yohannes Setegne (ETH) 6-0 6-0
Bosnia/Herzegovina defeated San Marino 3-0
Eldar Mustafic (BIH) d. Cristian Rosti (SMR) 7-5 7-5
Merid Zahirovic (BIH) d. Domenico Vicini (SMR) 7-6(3) 7-6(5)
Haris Basalic/Eldar Mustafic (BIH) d. Gabriel Francini/Domenico Vicini (SMR) 6-2 6-0
Armenia defeated Ethiopia 2-1
Artak Aroutiounyan (ARM) d. Samuel Gabriel (ETH) 6-2 6-1
Yohannes Setegne (ETH) d. David Babayan (ARM) 6-4 6-3
Aroutiounyan/Anri Makichyan (ARM) d. Gabriel/Setegne (ETH) 6-4 6-2

*Final Positions: 1. Luxembourg, 2. Senegal, 3. Turkey, 4. FYR of Macedonia,
5. Bosnia/Herzegovina, 6. San Marino, 7. Armenia, 8. Ethiopia.*

Euro/African Zone B
May 19–25, Plovdiv, Bulgaria

Group A: Bulgaria, Estonia, Kenya, Malta
Group B: Algeria, Cameroon, Moldova, Monaco

GROUP A

May 21

Bulgaria defeated Malta 3-0
Ivan Keskinov (BUL) d. Mark Schembri (MLT) 6-1 6-1
Orlin Stanoytchev (BUL) d. Chris Gatt (MLT) 6-4 6-0
Ivo Bratanov/Ivailo Traykov (BUL) d. Gordon Asciak/Mark Schembri (MLT) 7-6(8) 6-3

Estonia defeated Kenya 2-1
Andrei Luzgin (EST) d. Allan Cooper (KEN) 6-2 6-1
Paul Wekesa (KEN) d. Rene Busch (EST) 6-1 6-2
Andrei Luzgin/Gert Vilms (EST) d. Allan Cooper/Paul Wekesa (KEN) 6-3 6-4

May 22

Bulgaria defeated Estonia 3-0
Ivan Keskinov (BUL) d. Andrei Luzgin (EST) 6-3 6-1
Orlin Stanoytchev (BUL) d. Rene Busch (EST) 6-0 6-2
Ivo Bratanov/Ivailo Traykov (BUL) d. Raigo Saluste/Gert Vilms (EST) 6-2 6-4
Kenya defeated Malta 2-1
Gordon Asciak (MLT) d. Norbert Oduor (KEN) 6-3 6-4
Paul Wekesa (KEN) d. Chris Gatt (MLT) 3-6 6-4 6-3
Allan Cooper/Norbert Oduor (KEN) d. Gordon Asciak/Mark Schembri (MLT) 6-4 6-2

May 23

Bulgaria defeated Kenya 3-0
Ivan Keskinov (BUL) d. Norbert Oduor (KEN) 6-2 6-4
Orlin Stanoytchev (BUL) d. Allan Cooper (KEN) 6-2 6-1
Ivo Bratanov/Ivailo Traykov (BUL) d. Allan Cooper/Norbert Oduor (KEN) 6-3 6-2
Estonia defeated Malta 2-1
Andrei Luzgin (EST) d. Gordon Asciak (MLT) 3-6 6-4 6-3
Chris Gatt (MLT) d. Rene Busch (EST) 6-3 6-3
Andrei Luzgin/Gert Vilms (EST) d. Gordon Asciak/Chris Gatt (MLT) 6-2 6-3

GROUP B

May 21

Monaco defeated Algeria 2-1
Christophe Bosio (MON) d. Mohamed Mahmoudi (ALG) 6-2 7-6(4)
Sebastien Graeff (MON) d. Nourredine Mahmoudi (ALG) 6-4 6-3
Noudjeim Hakimi/N. Mahmoudi (ALG) d. Christophe Boggetti/Graeff (MON) 7-6(4) 7-6(6)
Moldova defeated Cameroon 3-0
Oleg Sinic (MDA) d. Angelin Mvogo (CMR) 7-5 3-6 7-5
Iuri Gorban (MDA) d. Yann Auzoux (CMR) 6-3 6-0
Iuri Gorban/Oleg Sinic (MDA) d. Lionel Kemajou/Joseph Oyebog (CMR) 6-3 6-3

May 22

Moldova defeated Algeria 3-0
Oleg Sinic (MDA) d. Noudjeim Hakimi (ALG) 6-4 6-1
Iuri Gorban (MDA) d. Nourredine Mahmoudi (ALG) 6-3 6-3
Iuri Gorban/Oleg Sinic (MDA) d. Noudjeim Hakimi/Nourredine Mahmoudi (ALG) 6-3 6-4
Monaco defeated Cameroon 2-1
Joseph Oyebog (CMR) d. Christophe Bosio (MON) 4-6 6-3 7-5
Sebastien Graeff (MON) d. Angelin Mvogo (CMR) 6-1 6-2
Christophe Boggetti/Graeff (MON) d. Yann Auzoux/Joseph Oyebog (CMR) 6-4 3-6 16-14

May 23

Monaco defeated Moldova 3-0
Christophe Bosio (MON) d. Oleg Sinic (MDA) 7-5 5-7 6-4
Sebastien Graeff (MON) d. Iuri Gorban (MDA) 6-4 6-4
Christophe Boggetti/Jacques Vincileoni (MON) d. Evgueni Plougarev/Maxim Savitski (MDA) 6-1 6-1
Cameroon defeated Algeria 2-1
Joseph Oyebog (CMR) d. Noudjeim Hakimi (ALG) 6-0 6-2
Mohamed Mahmoudi (ALG) d. Yann Auzoux (CMR) 6-0 6-4
Lionel Kemajou/Oyebog (CMR) d. Hakimi/Mahmoudi (ALG) 6-1 6-4

SEMIFINALS

Bulgaria defeated Moldova 3-0
Ivan Keskinov (BUL) d. Oleg Sinic (MDA) 6-2 6-4
Orlin Stanoytchev (BUL) d. Iuri Gorban (MDA) 6-7(6) 6-4 6-3
Ivo Bratanov/Ivailo Traykov (BUL) d. Evgueni Plougarev/Maxim Savitski (MDA) 6-1 6-3
Monaco defeated Estonia 3-0
Christophe Bosio (MON) d. Andrei Luzgin (EST) 6-4 6-4
Sebastien Graeff (MON) d. Rene Busch (EST) 7-5 6-4
Christophe Boggetti/Jacques Vincileoni (MON) d. Raigo Saluste/Gert Vilms (EST) 7-6(5) 7-6(5)

FINAL

Bulgaria defeated Monaco 3-0
Ivan Keskinov (BUL) d. Christophe Bosio (MON) 7-5 6-4
Orlin Stanoytchev (BUL) d. Sebastien Graeff (MON) 6-3 4-6 6-3
Ivo Bratanov/Ivailo Traykov (BUL) d. Christophe Boggetti/Graeff (MON) 6-7(6) 6-2 6-1

PLAYOFF FOR 3RD/4TH POSITIONS

Estonia defeated Moldova 2-1
Oleg Sinic (MDA) d. Gert Vilms (EST) 6-1 6-3
Rene Busch (EST) d. Iuri Gorban (MDA) 3-6 6-4 6-1
Andrei Luzgin/Gert Vilms (EST) d. Iuri Gorban/Oleg Sinic (MDA) 6-2 6-3

PLAYOFFS FOR 5TH – 8TH POSITIONS

Malta defeated Cameroon 2-1
Mark Schembri (MLT) d. Joseph Oyebog (CMR) 7-6(9) 3-6 6-4
Angelin Mvogo (CMR) d. Chris Gatt (MLT) 6-3 6-3
Gordon Asciak/Mark Schembri (MLT) d. Yann Auzoux/Angelin Mvogo (CMR) 7-6(4) 6-3
Kenya defeated Algeria 2-1
Mohamed Mahmoudi (ALG) d. Allan Cooper (KEN) 4-6 6-3 6-3
Paul Wekesa (KEN) d. Nourredine Mahmoudi (ALG) 6-3 3-6 6-3
Cooper/Norbert Oduor (KEN) d. Noudjeim Hakimi/M. Mahmoudi (ALG) 5-7 6-4 6-4
Kenya defeated Malta 2-1
Allan Cooper (KEN) d. Gordon Asciak (MLT) 6-4 6-2
Paul Wekesa (KEN) d. Mark Schembri (MLT) 6-3 4-6 6-2
Gordon Asciak/Chris Gatt (MLT) d. Allan Cooper/Norbert Oduor (KEN) w/o

PLAYOFF FOR 7TH/8TH POSITIONS

Algeria defeated Cameroon 2-1
Angelin Mvogo (CMR) d. Mohamed Mahmoudi (ALG) 6-0 0-0 (30-0) ret.
Nourredine Mahmoudi (ALG) d. Yann Auzoux (CMR) 6-0 6-1
Noudjeim Hakimi/N. Mahmoudi (ALG) d. Auzoux/Mvogo (CMR) 3-6 7-6(7) 6-1

Final Positions: 1. Bulgaria, 2. Monaco, 3. Estonia, 4. Moldova, 5. Kenya, 6. Malta, 7. Algeria, 8. Cameroon.

Asia/Oceania Zone
26-30 March 26–30, Doha, Qatar

Group A: Kazakhstan, Kuwait, Bahrain, Bangladesh
Group B: Pacific Oceania, Qatar, Sri Lanka, Malaysia

GROUP A

March 26

Kazakhstan defeated Bahrain 2-1
Alexei Kedriouk (KAZ) d. Essam Abdul-Aal (BRN) 7-6(5) 6-4
Abdul Shehab (BRN) d. Igor Chaldounov (KAZ) 6-4 6-2
Igor Chaldounov/Kedriouk (KAZ) d. Essam Abdul-Aal/Nader Abdul-Aal (BRN) 7-5 4-6 7-5
Kuwait defeated Bangladesh 3-0
Mohammed Al-Foudari (KUW) d. Hira-Lal Rahman (BAN) 6-4 6-4
Adel Al-Shatti (KUW) d. Shovon Jamaly (BAN) 6-4 6-3
Khalid Al-Gharabally/Mohammed Ghareeb (KUW) d. Jamaly/Rahman (BAN) 7-6(1) 6-4

March 27

Kazakhstan defeated Bangladesh 3-0
Alexei Kedriouk (KAZ) d. Hira-Lal Rahman (BAN) 6-2 6-2
Igor Chaldounov (KAZ) d. Dilip Passia (BAN) 4-6 6-4 6-2
Jouri Karlov/Kedriouk (KAZ) d. Shovon Jamaly/Dilip Passia (BAN) 6-2 6-4
Kuwait defeated Bahrain 2-1
Essam Abdul-Aal (BRN) d. Mohammad Ghareeb (KUW) 6-3 6-0
Adel Al-Shatti (KUW) d. Abdul Shehab (BRN) 6-2 6-1
Khalid Al-Gharabally/Al-Shatti (KUW) d. E. Abdul-Aal/N. Abdul-Aal (BRN) 3-6 7-5 6-2

March 28

Kazakhstan defeated Kuwait 2-1
Alexei Kedriouk (KAZ) d. Mohammad Al Foudari (KUW) 6-2 6-3
Mohammed Ghareeb (KUW) d. Igor Chaldounov (KAZ) 6-1 6-4
Chaldounov/Kedriouk (KAZ) d. Al-Foudari/Khalid Al-Gharabally (KUW) 6-2 6-3
Bahrain defeated Bangladesh 2-1
Shehab Shehab (BRN) d. Tofazzal Hossain (BAN) 6-3 6-1
Dilip Passia (BAN) d. Abdul Shehab (BRN) 6-2 7-6(1)
Nader Abdul-Aal/Abdul Shehab (BRN) d. Shovon Jamaly/Hira-Lal Rahman (BAN) 6-3 6-3

GROUP B

March 26

Qatar defeated Malaysia 2-1
Vasuthevan Ortchuan (MAS) d. Nasser Al-Khulaifi (QAT) 6-2 1-6 6-2
Sultan Al-Alawi (QAT) d. Ramayah Ramachandran (MAS) 2-6 6-3 6-2
Al-Alawi/Al-Khulaifi (QAT) d. Ramachandran/Abdul-Aziz Shazali (MAS) 6-2 6-3.
Pacific Oceania defeated Sri Lanka 2-1
Rohan De Silva (SRI) d. Motuliki Kailahi (POC) 6-3 6-3
Lency Tenai (POC) d. Jayendra Wijeyesekera (SRI) 4-6 7-6(2) 6-1
Kailahi/Tenai (POC) d. De Silva/Wijeyesekera (SRI) 7-6(4) 3-6 6-3.

March 27

Malaysia defeated Pacific Oceania 2-1
Vasuthevan Ortchuan (MAS) d. Motuliki Kailahi (POC) 6-4 6-3
Ramayah Ramachandran (MAS) d. Lency Tenai (POC) 6-0 6-1
Kailahi/Tenai (POC) d. Jamal Mulyadi/Ramachandran (MAS) 7-6(3) 3-6 6-3
Qatar defeated Sri Lanka 2-1
Nasser Al-Khulaifi (QAT) d. Rohan De Silva (SRI) 6-2 6-7(5) 8-6
Sultan Al-Alawi (QAT) Jayendra Wijeyesekera (SRI) 7-5 6-1
De Silva/Wijeyesekera (SRI) d. Mohamed-Ali Al-Saoud/Cesarito Diong (QAT) 6-2 7-5

March 28

Sri Lanka defeated Malaysia 3-0
Rohan De Silva (SRI) d. Vasuthevan Ortchuan (MAS) 7-6(1) 6-0
Jayendra Wijeyesekera (SRI) d. Ramayah Ramachandran (MAS) 7-6(6) 5-7 6-4
De Silva/Wijeyesekera (SRI) d. Jamal Mulyadi/Ramachandran (MAS) 6-3 6-2
Pacific Oceania defeated Qatar 2-1
Motuliki Kailahi (POC) d. Mohamed-Ali Al-Saoud (QAT) 4-6 6-2 6-3
Sultan Al-Alawi (QAT) d. Lency Tenai (POC) 6-1 6-2
Motuliki Kailahi/Lency Tenai (POC) d. Sultan Al-Alawi/Nasser Al-Khulaifi (QAT) 4-6 6-4 6-2

SEMIFINALS

Pacific Oceania defeated Kuwait 2-1
Motuliki Kailahi (POC) d. Mohammad Al-Foudari (KUW) 6-3 6-2
Adel Al-Shatti (KUW) d. Lency Tenai (POC) 2-6 6-2 6-0
Kailahi/Tenai (POC) d. Khalid Al-Gharabally/Al-Shatti (KUW) 1-6 6-2 6-2
Qatar defeated Kazakhstan 2-1
Alexei Kedriouk (KAZ) d. Nasser Al-Khulaifi (QAT) 6-2 6-2
Sultan Al-Alawi (QAT) d. Igor Chaldounov (KAZ) 6-0 6-3
Al-Alawi/Cesarito Diong (QAT) d. Chaldounov/Kedriouk (KAZ) 6-2 6-4

FINAL

Qatar defeated Pacific Oceania 2-1
Motuliki Kailahi (POC) d. Cesarito Diong (QAT) 7-6(4) ret.
Sultan Al-Alawi (QAT) d. Lency Tenai (POC) 6-2 6-3
Sultan Al-Alawi/Nasser Al-Khulaifi (QAT) d. Motuliki Kailahi/Lency Tenai (POC) 2-6 6-3 6-2.

PLAYOFF FOR 3RD/4TH POSITIONS

Kazakhstan defeated Kuwait 3-0
Alexei Kedriouk (KAZ) d. Mohammed Al-Foudari (KUW) 3-0 ret.
Igor Chaldounov (KAZ) d. Khalid Al-Gharabally (KUW) 6-3 0-0(40-0) ret.
Chaldounov/Kedriouk (KAZ) d. MAl-Foudari/Al-Gharabally (KUW) walkover

PLAYOFFS FOR 5TH – 8TH POSITIONS

Malaysia defeated Bahrain 2-1
Essam Abdul-Aal (BRN) d. Vasuthevan Ortchuan (MAS) 7-5 6-3
Ramayah Ramachandran (MAS) d. Abdul Shehab (BRN) 6-1 6-0
Jamal Mulyadi/RRamachandran (MAS) d. Nader Abdul-Aal/Shehab Shehab (BRN) 6-0 6-2
Sri Lanka defeated Bangladesh 2-1
Rohan De Silva (SRI) d. Dilip Passia (BAN) 5-7 6-4 6-1
Shovon Jamaly (BAN) d. Jayendra Wijeyesekera (SRI) 2-6 6-4 6-2
De Silva/Wijeyesekera (SRI) d. Jamaly/Passia (BAN) 3-6 6-4 6-4
Malaysia defeated Sri Lanka 3-0
Vasuthevan Ortchuan (MAS) d. Lahiru Jayasuriya (SRI) 6-4 7-6(3)
Ramayah Ramachandran (MAS) d. Roshan Razik (SRI) 6-1 6-1
Jamal Mulyadi/Abdul-Aziz Shazali (MAS) d. Rohan De Silva/Jayendra Wijeyesekera (SRI) 4-6 6-4 6-2
Bahrain defeated Bangladesh 2-1
Essam Abdul-Aal (BRN) d. Dilip Passia (BAN) 6-2 6-1
Shovon Jamaly (BAN) d. Abdul Shehab (BRN) 6-1 6-4
Nader Abdul-Aal/Shehab Shehab (BRN) d. Shovon Jamaly/Dilip Passia (BAN) 6-2 1-6 6-4

***Final Positions: 1. Qatar, 2. Pacific Oceania, 3. Kazakhstan. 4. Kuwait, 5. Malaysia,
6. Sri Lanka, 7. Bahrain, 8. Bangladesh***

American Zone
27 Apri 27–May 3, Southampton, Bermuda

Group A: Antigua/Barbuda, Barbados, Panama, Trinidad & Tobago
Group B: Bolivia, Dominican Republic, Guatemala, Jamaica

GROUP A

April 29

Antigua/Barbuda defeated Trinidad & Tobago 3-0
Fitzroy Anthony (ANT) d. Simon Evelyn (TRI) 6-7(5) 7-5 6-3
Phillip Williamson (ANT) d. Orville Adams (TRI) 7-5 6-2
John Maginley/Phillip Williamson (ANT) d. Simon Evelyn/Ivor Grazette (TRI) 6-3 6-2
Panama defeated Barbados 2-1
Juan-Pablo Herrera (PAN) d. James Betts (BAR) 6-1 6-3
Chad Valdez (PAN) d. Bernard Frost (BAR) 6-3 6-1
James Betts/Bernard Frost (BAR) d. Jan Gelabert/John Silva (PAN) 6-7(5) 6-4 6-2

April 30

Antigua/Barbuda defeated Barbados 2-1
James Betts (BAR) d. Fitzroy Anthony (ANT) 6-1 3-6 6-3
Phillip Williamson (ANT) d. Bernard Frost (BAR) 6-3 6-4
John Maginley/Phillip Williamson (ANT) d. James Betts/Bernard Frost (BAR) 6-0 6-4
Panama defeated Trinidad & Tobago 3-0
Juan-Pablo Herrera (PAN) d. Simon Evelyn (TRI) 6-1 6-3
Chad Valdez (PAN) d. Orville Adams (TRI) 7-6(5) 6-1
Jan Gelabert/John Silva (PAN) d. Ivor Grazette/Ronald Greaves 6-7(1) 7-6(5) 6-4

May 1

Panama defeated Antigua/Barbuda 2-1
Juan Pablo Herrera (PAN) d. Fitzroy Anthony (ANT) 6-3 6-4
Phillip Williamson (ANT) d. Chad Valdez (PAN) 6-1 1-6 8-6
Jan Gelabert/Juan Pablo-Herrera (PAN) d. Fitzroy Anthony/John Maginley (ANT) 6-3 6-4
Trinidad & Tobago defeated Barbados 2-1
Ivor Grazette (TRI) d. James Betts (BAR) 6-1 2-6 6-1
Bernard Frost (BAR) d. Simon Evelyn (TRI) 6-4 7-5
Ivor Grazette/Ronald Greaves (TRI) d. Craig Smith/Duane Williams (BAR) 6-4 4-6 6-2

GROUP B

April 29

Guatemala defeated Jamaica 2-1
Andres Asturias (GUA) d. Jermaine Smith (JAM) 7-6(2) 6-4
Daniel Chavez (GUA) d. Nicholas Malcolm (JAM) 6-0 6-3
Elvis Henry/Nicholas Malcolm (JAM) d. Luis Perez-Chete/Luis Valencia (GUA) 6-3 3-6 8-6.
Bolivia defeated Dominican Republic 2-1
Carlos Navarro (BOL) d. Sixto Camacho (DOM) 2-6 7-6(4) 6-3
Rodrigo Vallejo (DOM) d. Pablo Ugarte (BOL) 6-4 6-2
Navarro/Pablo Ugarte (BOL) d. Camacho/Vallejo (DOM) 6-7(4) 6-2 6-2

April 30

Dominican Republic defeated Guatemala 2-1
Andres Asturias (GUA) d. Jorge Duenas (DOM) 7-5 6-2
Rodrigo Vallejo (DOM) d. Daniel Chavez (GUA) 7-5 6-3
Sixto Camacho/Jorge Duenas (DOM) d. Andres Asturias/Luis Perez-Chete (GUA) 7-6(5) 6-4
Jamaica defeated Bolivia 3-0
Jessie Smatt (JAM) d. Carlos Navarro (BOL) 6-2 6-2
Jermaine Smith (JAM) d. Pablo Ugarte (BOL) 6-4 6-4
Elvis Henry/Nicholas Malcolm (JAM) d. Eduardo Kohlberg/Navarro (BOL) 6-7(5) 6-2 6-2

May 1

Jamaica defeated Dominican Republic 2-1
Jessie Smatt (JAM) d. Jorge Duenas (DOM) 6-3 6-4
Rodrigo Vallejo (DOM) d. Jermaine Smith (JAM) 7-6(5) 6-4
Nicholas Malcolm/Smith (JAM) d. Sixto Camacho/Vallejo (DOM) 6-1 3-6 6-3
Guatemala defeated Bolivia 3-0
Andrea Asturias (GUA) d. Carlos Navarro (BOL) 6-4 6-4
Daniel Chavez (GUA) d. Pablo Ugarte (BOL) 7-5 2-6 7-5
Luis Perez-Chete/Luis Valencia (GUA) d. Eduardo Kohlberg/Carlos Navarro (BOL) 6-4 6-1

SEMIFINALS

Jamaica defeated Panama 3-0
Jessie Smatt (JAM) d. Juan-Pablo Herrera (PAN) 6-4 2-6 6-2
Jermaine Smith (JAM) d. Chad Valdez (PAN) 5-7 7-5 6-4
Elvis Henry/ Nicholas Malcolm (JAM) d. Jan Gelabert/John Silva (PAN) 6-3 6-3
Guatemala defeated Antigua/Barbuda 2-1
Andres Asturias (GUA) d. Fitzroy Anthony (ANT) 6-3 6-1
Phillip Williamson (ANT) d. Daniel Chavez (GUA) 6-3 6-7(2) 6-2
Asturias/Luis Perez-Chete (GUA) d. John Maginley/Phillip Williamson (ANT) 6-3 5-7 6-4
Dominican Republic defeated Trinidad & Tobago 3-0
Sixto Camacho (DOM) d. Ivor Grazette (TRI) 6-4 6-2
Rodrigo Vallejo (DOM) d. Simon Evelyn (TRI) 6-3 6-3
Sixto Camacho/Jorge Duenas (DOM) d. Ivor Grazette/Ronald Greaves (TRI) 7-5 6-3
Bolivia defeated Barbados 2-1
Carlos Navarro (BOL) d. James Betts (BAR) 6-3 6-3
Pablo Ugarte (BOL) d. Bernard Frost (BAR) 4-6 6-0 6-1
James Betts/Duane Williams (BAR) d. Eduardo Kohlberg/Pablo Ugarte (BOL) 2-6 6-4 6-3

FINAL

Guatemala defeated Jamaica 3-0
Andres Asturias (GUA) d. Jessie Smatt (JAM) 6-0 5-7 6-4
Daniel Chavez (GUA) d. Jermaine Smith (JAM) 7-5 6-1
Daniel Chavez/Luis Perez-Chete (GUA) d. Nicholas Malcolm/Elvis Henry (JAM) 7-6(4) 6-1

PLAYOFF FOR 3RD/4TH POSITIONS

Antigua/Barbuda defeated Panama 2-1
Juan-Pablo Herrera (PAN) d. John Maginley (ANT) 6-2 6-0
Phillip Williamson (ANT) d. Chad Valdez (PAN) 6-4 6-1
Fitzroy Anthony/Williamson (ANT) d. Jan Gelabert/Herrera (PAN) 3-6 6-3 6-0

PLAYOFF FOR 5TH/6TH POSITIONS

Dominican Republic defeated Bolivia 2-1
Carlos Navarro (BOL) d. Jorge Duenas (DOM) 2-6 7-5 6-1
Rodrigo Vallejo (DOM) d. Pablo Ugarte (BOL) 5-7 6-4 6-1
Sixto Camacho/Vallejo (DOM) d. Navarro/Ugarte (BOL) 6-4 6-7(5) 6-4

PLAYOFF FOR 7TH/8TH POSITIONS

Barbados defeated Trinidad & Tobago 2-1
Duane Williams (BAR) d. Ivor Grazette (TRI) 6-4 7-6(4)
James Betts (BAR) d. Orville Adams (TRI) 3-5 Ret
Ronald Greaves/Simon Evelyn (TRI) d. James Betts/Duane Williams (BAR) 6-2 7-5

Final Positions: 1. Guatemala, 2. Jamaica, 3. Antigua/Barbuda, 4. Panama,
5. Dominican Republic, 6. Bolivia, 7. Barbados, 8. Trinidad & Tobago

Group IV

Euro/African Zone A
March 19–23, Gaborone, Botswana

Group A: Liechtenstein, Sudan, Togo, Uganda
Group B: Botswana, Djibouti, Iceland, Madagascar

GROUP A

March 19

Liechtenstein defeated Sudan 3-0
Jurgen Tomordy (LIE) d. Mandour Abdalla (SUD) 6-2 6-3
Stephan Ritter (LIE) d. Asim El Agraa (SUD) 6-2 6-0
Hartmut Birkner/Roland Buchel (LIE) d. Abbas Jeha/Abdalla Jeha (SUD) 6-3 6-3
Togo defeated Uganda 3-0
Kodjo Apeti (TOG) d. Renato Sebbi (UGA) 6-2 6-2
Jean Loglo (TOG) d. John Oduke (UGA) 6-1 6-4
Kossi Loglo/Midodji Segbeaya (TOG) d. Christopher Bagala/ Renato Sebbi (UGA) 6-1 6-2.

March 20

Liechtenstein defeated Uganda 3-0
Jurgen Tomordy (LIE) d. Erick Ofuyulu (UGA) 6-2 6-3
Stephan Ritter (LIE) d. John Oduke (UGA) 6-3 7-5
Hartmut Birkner/Roland Buchel (LIE) d. Christopher Bagala/Renato Sebbi (UGA) 7-6(4) 4-6 10-8

Togo defeated Sudan 3-0
Kodjo Apeti (TOG) d. Mandour Abdalla (SUD) 7-5 6-1
Jean Loglo (TOG) d. Asim El Agraa (SUD) 6-2 6-0
Kossi Loglo/Midodji Segbeaya (TOG) d. Mandour Abdalla/Abbas Jeha (SUD) 6-1 7-5

March 21

Togo defeated Liechtenstein 3-0
Kodjo Apeti (TOG) d. Roland Buchel (LIE) 6-0 6-0
Jean Loglo (TOG) d. Hartmut Birkner (LIE) 6-2 6-0
Kossi Loglo/ Midodji Segbeaya (TOG) d. Birkner/Buchel (LIE) 6-4 6-3
Uganda defeated Sudan 2-1
Mandour Abdalla (SUD) d. Renato Sebbi (UGA) 6-3 6-1
John Oduke (UGA) d. Asim El Agraa (SUD) 6-1 6-2
John Oduke/Renato Sebbi (UGA) d. Mandour Abdalla/Asim El Agraa (SUD)75 6-3

GROUP B

March 19

Botswana defeated Djibouti 3-0
Gavin Jeftha (BOT) d. Omar Mohammed (DJI) 6-0 6-0
Petrus Molefhe (BOT) d. Abdul Moussa (DJI) 6-0 6-0
Michael Judd/Thato Kgosimore (BOT) d. Ali Aden/Chamsan Nasser-Saeed (DJI) 6-2 6-1
Madagascar defeated Iceland 3-0
Harivony Andrianafetra (MAD) d. Einar Sigurgeirsson (ISL) 6-0 6-1
Rija Rajoabelina (MAD) d. Gunnar Einarsson (ISL) 6-4 6-4
Andrianafetra/Donne Radison (MAD) d. Stefan Palsson/Olafur Sveinsson (ISL) 6-2 6-0

March 20

Madagascar defeated Botswana 2-1
Harivony Andrianafetra (MAD) d. Gavin Jeftha (BOT) 6-2 6-4
Petrus Molefhe (BOT) d. Rija Rajoabelina (MAD) 7-6(5) 7-5
Andrianafetra/Rajoabelina (MAD) d. Thato Kgosimore/Molefhe (BOT) 6-1 6-3
Iceland defeated Djibouti 3-0
Einar Sigurgeirsson (ISL) d. Ali Aden (DJI) 6-0 6-0
Gunnar Einarsson (ISL) d. Chamsan Nasser-Saeed (DJI) 6-0 6-0
Gunnar Einarsson/Stefan Palsson (ISL) d. Omar Mohammed /Abdul Moussa (DJI) 6-2 6-1

March 21

Botswana defeated Iceland 2-1
Gavin Jeftha (BOT) d. Einar Sigurgeirsson (ISL) 6-1 6-3
Petrus Molefhe (BOT) d. Gunnar Einarsson (ISL) 7-6(4) ret.
Stefan Palsson/Sigurgeirsson (ISL) d. Michael Judd/Thato Kgosimore (BOT) 7-6(4) 6-3
Madagascar defeated Djibouti 3-0
Jean Rakotondravelo (MAD) d. Ali Aden (DJI) 6-0 6-0
Donne Radison (MAD) d. Omar Mohammed (DJI) 6-0 6-2
Radison/Rakotondravelo (MAD) d. Abdul Moussa/Chamsan Nasser-Saeed (DJI) 6-0 6-0

SEMIFINALS

Togo defeated Botswana 2-1
Gavin Jeftha (BOT) d. Kodjo Apeti (TOG) 6-3 6-4
Jean Loglo (TOG) d. Petrus Molefhe (BOT) 6-4 7-5
Kodjo Apeti/Jean Loglo (TOG) d. Michael Judd/Thato Kgosimore (BOT) 6-3 6-4
Madagascar defeated Liechtenstein 3-0
Harivony Andrianafetra (MAD) d. Jurgen Tomordy (LIE) 6-7(4) 6-1 6-2
Rija Rajoabelina (MAD) d. Stephan Ritter (LIE) 6-4 6-3
Donne Radison/Jean Rakotondravelo (MAD) d. Hartmut Birkner/Roland Buchel (LIE) 6-1 6-1

FINAL

Madagascar defeated Togo 2-1
Harivony Andrianafetra (MAD) d. Kodjo Apeti (TOG) 6-2 6-3
Jean Loglo (TOG) d. Rija Rajoabelina (MAD) 6-2 6-3
Harivony Andrianafetra/Rija Rajoabelina (MAD) d. Kodjo Apeti/Jean Loglo (TOG)75 6-3

PLAYOFF FOR 3RD/4TH POSITIONS

Liechtenstein defeated Botswana 2-1
Jurgen Tomordy (LIE) d. Thato Kgosimore (BOT) 7-5 6-3
Petrus Molefhe (BOT) d. Stephan Ritter (LIE) 3-6 6-3 6-0
Stephan Ritter/Jurgen Tomordy (LIE) d. Gavin Jeftha/Michael Judd (BOT) walkover.

PLAYOFFS FOR 5TH – 8TH POSITIONS

Uganda defeated Djibouti 3-0
Renato Sebbi (UGA) d. Ali Aden (DJI) 6-0 6-1
John Oduke (UGA) d. Omar Mohammed (DJI) 6-0 6-0
John Oduke/Renato Sebbi (UGA) d. Ali Aden/Omar Mohammed (DJI) 6-0 6-1.
Sudan defeated Iceland 2-1
Mandour Abdalla (SUD) d. Stefan Palsson (ISL) 6-2 6-4
Gunnar Einarsson (ISL) d. Asim El Agraa (SUD) 6-2 5-7 6-3
Mandour Abdalla /Abbas Jeha (SUD) d. Palsson/Einar Sigurgeirsson (ISL) 3-6 6-2 7-5
Uganda defeated Sudan 2-1
Mandour Abdalla (SUD) d. Renato Sebbi (UGA) 6-3 6-3
John Oduke (UGA) d. Asim El Agraa (SUD) 6-2 6-2
John Oduke/Renato Sebbi (UGA) d. Mandour Abdalla/Abbas Jeha (SUD) 6-4 3-6 6-4
Iceland defeated Djibouti 3-0
Einar Sigurgeirsson (ISL) d. Ali Aden (DJI) 6-0 6-2
Gunnar Einarsson (ISL) d. Omar Mohammed (DJI) 6-3 6-1
Gunnar Einarsson/Einar Sigurgeirsson (ISL) d. Ali Aden/Omar Mohammed (DJI) 6-1 6-1

Final Positions: 1. Madagascar, 2. Togo, 3. Liechtenstein, 4. Botswana, 5. Uganda, 6. Sudan, 7. Iceland, 8. Djibouti.

Euro/African Zone B
May 19–25, Nicosia, Cyprus

May 21

Cyprus defeated Congo 3-0
Marinos Baghdatis (CYP) d. Chatrian Gnitou (CGO) 6-4 6-0
Demetrios Leondis (CYP) d. Alain Bemba (CGO) 6-1 6-1
Leondis/Neoklis Neokleous (CYP) d. Martial Banguid/Gnitou (CGO) 6-2 6-1
Tunisia defeated Benin 3-0
Sami Sidia (TUN) d. Alphonse Gandonou (BEN) 6-1 6-4
Oualid Jellali (TUN) d. Christophe Pognon (BEN) 6-1 7-5
Oualid Jellali/Sami Sidia (TUN) d. Jean-Marie Da Silva/Alphonse Gandonou (BEN) 6-1 6-2
Zambia defeated Azerbaijan 3-0
Kachinga Sinkala (ZAM) d. Dmitri Zaraubin (AZE) 6-2 6-0
Lighton Ndefway (ZAM) d. Igor Barisov (AZE) 6-3 6-3
Sidney Bwalya/Lawrence Chileshe (ZAM) d. Raouf Eyvazov/Zaraubin (AZE) 6-0 10 ret.

May 22

Cyprus defeated Zambia 2-1
Marinos Baghdatis (CYP) d. Kachinga Sinkala (ZAM) 6-4 6-4
Demetrios Leondis (CYP) d. Lighton Ndefway (ZAM) 6-3 6-4
Sidney Bwalya/Ndefway (ZAM) d. Demetrios Leondis/Neoklis Neokleous (CYP) 7-5 6-2
Tunisia defeated Azerbaijan 3-0
Sami Sidia (TUN) d. Dmitri Zaraubin (AZE) 6-1 6-0
Oualid Jellali (TUN) d. Igor Barisov (AZE) 6-2 6-1
Oualid Jellali/Sami Sidia (TUN) d. Igor Barisov/Dmitri Zaraubin (AZE) 6-1 6-2
Benin defeated Congo 3-0
Alphonse Gandonou (BEN) d. Martial Banguid (CGO) 6-2 6-0
Christophe Pognon (BEN) d. Chatrian Gnitou (CGO) 6-3 6-1
Jean-Marie Da Silva/Gandonou (BEN) d. Alain Bemba/Gnitou (CGO) 6-4 6-1

May 23

Tunisia defeated Congo 3-0
Sami Sidia (TUN) d. Pagnol Madzou (CGO) 6-1 6-1
Oualid Jellali (TUN) d. Martial Banguid (CGO) 6-0 6-1
Oualid Jellali/Sami Sidia (TUN) d. Alain Bemba/Chatrian Gnitou (CGO) 6-0 6-1
Cyprus defeated Azerbaijan 3-0
Marinos Baghdatis (CYP) d. Dmitri Zaraubin (AZE) 6-1 6-4
Demetrios Leondis (CYP) d. Igor Barisov (AZE) 6-2 6-1
Demetrios Leondis/Neoklis Neokleous (CYP) d. Igor Barisov/Dmitri Zaraubin (AZE) 6-4 6-4.
Benin defeated Zambia 2-1
Alphonse Gandonou (BEN) d. Kachinga Sinkala (ZAM) 6-4 6-1
Christophe Pognon (BEN) d. Lighton Ndefway (ZAM) 6-4 6-2
Sidney Bwalya/Lawrence Chileshe (ZAM) d. Jean-Marie Da Silva/Gandonou (BEN) 6-3 7-5

May 24

Cyprus defeated Benin 2-1
Marinos Baghdatis (CYP) d. Alphonse Gandonou (BEN) 6-3 6-3
Christophe Pognon (BEN) d. Demetrios Leondis (CYP) 6-4 6-3
Leondis/Neoklis Neokleous (CYP) d. Jean-Marie Da Silva/Gandonou (BEN) 6-3 7-6(6)
Tunisia defeated Zambia 2-1
Sami Sidia (TUN) d. Sidney Bwalya (ZAM) 6-2 7-5
Oualid Jellali (TUN) d. Lighton Ndefway (ZAM) 6-1 6-3
Bwalya/Kachinga Sinkala (ZAM) d. Selim Belhadj-Ali/Jellali (TUN) 4-6 6-4 6-4

Azerbaijan defeated Congo 2-1
Dmitri Zaraubin (AZE) d. Martial Banguid (CGO) 3-6 6-1 6-0
Alain Bemba (CGO) d. Igor Barisov (AZE) 6-2 6-1
Igor Barisov/Dmitri Zaraubin (AZE) d. Martial Banguid/Alain Bemba (CGO) 6-2 6-3

May 25

Tunisia defeated Cyprus 2-1
Sami Sidia (TUN) d. Marinos Baghdatis (CYP) 1-6 6-4 6-4
Demetrios Leondis (CYP) d. Oualid Jellali (TUN) 6-3 6-1
Oualid Jellali/Sami Sidia (TUN) d. Demetrios Leondis/Neoklis Neokleous (CYP) 6-4 6-3.
Zambia defeated Congo 3-0
Sidney Bwalya (ZAM) d. Pagnol Madzou (CGO) 6-0 6-0
Lighton Ndefway (ZAM) d. Chatrian Gnitou (CGO) 6-0 6-1
Lawrence Chileshe/ Kachinga Sinkala (ZAM) d. Martial Banguid/Gnitou (CGO) 6-2 6-4
Benin defeated Azerbaijan 3-0
Alphonse Gandonou (BEN) d. Farid Jafarov (AZE) 6-0 6-0
Christophe Pognon (BEN) d. Dmitri Zaraubin (AZE) 6-1 6-3
Jean-Marie Da Silva/Alphonse Gandonou (BEN) d. Igor Barisov/Raouf Eyvazov (AZE) w/o

Final Positions: 1. Tunisia, 2. Cyprus, 3. Benin, 4. Zambia, 5. Azerbaijan, 6. Congo

Asia/Oceania Group
March 26-30, Muscat, Oman

March 26
No play due to rain

March 27

Syria defeated United Arab Emirates 3-0
Rabi Bou-Hassoun (SYR) d. Mahmoud Nader (UAE) 6-2 6-2
Dawood Dawoodian (SYR) d. Saeed Al-Maktoum (UAE) 6-2 6-4
Abdul Salim/Lais Salim (SYR) d. Othman Al-Ulama/Mahmoud Nader (UAE)75 6-2
Tajikistan defeated Jordan 2-1
Fares Azzouni (JOR) d. Sergei Makashin (TJK) 6-2 6-2
Mansour Yakhyaev (TJK) d. Ahmed Al-Hadid (JOR) 6-0 6-0
Bakhrullo Radjabalien/Yakhyaev (TJK) d. Azzouni/Ghassan Hassan-Qadi (JOR) 6-1 6-0
Oman defeated Brunei 2-1
Ismasufian Ibrahim (BRU) d. Fahad Al-Hashmi (OMA) 6-3 6-1
Mudrik Al-Rawahi (OMA) d. Pheng-Chai Chua (BRU) 6-0 6-0
Khalid Al-Nabhani/Al-Rawahi (OMA) d. Pheng-Chai Chua/Ibrahim (BRU) 4-6 7-5 7-5

March 28
First Session

Syria defeated Tajikistan 2-1
Rabi Bou-Hassoun (SYR) d. Sergei Makashin (TJK) 6-3 7-5
Mansour Yakhyaev (TJK) d. Dawood Dawoodian (SYR) 6-2 6-4
Bou-Hassoun/Dawoodian (SYR) d. Bakhrullo Radjabalien/Yakhyaev (TJK) 6-3 7-6(5)
United Arab Emirates defeated Brunei 2-1
Omar Bahrouzyan (UAE) d. Ismasufian Ibrahim (BRU) 6-3 6-2
Othman Al-Ulama (UAE) d. Pheng-Chai Chua (BRU) 6-2 7-6(3)
Felix Chin/Ibrahim (BRU) d. Saeed Al-Maktoum/Mahmoud Nader (UAE) 6-3 6-4
Oman defeated Jordan 2-1
 Fares Azzouni (JOR) d. Fahad Al-Hashmi (OMA) 6-0 7-5
Mudrik Al-Rawahi (OMA) d. Ahmed Al-Hadid (JOR) 6-1 6-2
Khalid Al-Nabhani/Al-Rawahi (OMA) d. Fares Azzouni/Ghassan Hassan-Qadi (JOR) 6-3 6-4

March 28
Second Session

Tajikistan defeated Oman 3-0
Sergei Makashin (TJK) d. Fahad Al-Hashmi (OMA) 6-1 6-0
Mansour Yakhyaev (TJK) d. Mudrik Al-Rawahi (OMA) 6-0 6-0
Bakhrullo Radjabalien/Yakhyaev (TJK) d. Khalid Al-Nabhani/Mudrik Al-Rawahi (OMA) 6-3 6-0
United Arab Emirates defeated Jordan 2-1
Omar Bahrouzyan (UAE) d. Fares Azzouni (JOR) 7-5 4-6 6-3
Othman Al-Ulama (UAE) d. Ghassan Hassan-Qadi (JOR) 6-2 3-6 6-2
Tharwat Al-Quasi/Hassan-Qadi (JOR) d. Saeed Al-Maktoum/Mahmoud Nader (UAE) 6-3 6-1
Syria defeated Brunei 3-0
Rabi Bou-Hassoun (SYR) d. Fauzan Sulaiman (BRU) 6-0 6-2
Dawood Dawoodian (SYR) d. Felix Chin (BRU) 6-0 6-3
Abdul Salim/Lais Salim (SYR) d. Pheng-Chai Chua/Ismasufian Ibrahim (BRU) 2-6 6-0 6-3

March 29

Brunei defeated Jordan 2-1
Ismasufian Ibrahim (BRU) d. Tharwat Al-Quasi (JOR) 6-2 6-2
Fares Azzouni (JOR) d. Felix Chin (BRU) 7-5 6-0
Pheng-Chai Chua/Ibrahim (BRU) d. Azzouni/Ghassan Hassan-Qadi (JOR) 6-1 7-5
Tajikistan defeated United Arab Emirates 3-0
Sergei Makashin (TJK) d. Omar Bahrouzyan (UAE) 6-3 6-4
Mansour Yakhyaev (TJK) d. Othman Al-Ulama (UAE) 6-1 6-1
Makashin/Yakhyaev (TJK) d. Saeed Al-Maktoum/Mahmoud Nader (UAE) 6-1 6-3
Syria defeated Oman 3-0
Rabi Bou-Hassoun (SYR) d. Khalid Al-Nabhani (OMA) 6-0 6-1
Lais Salim (SYR) d. Mudrik Al-Rawahi (OMA) 6-3 7-6(2)
Abdul Salim/Lais Salim (SYR) d. Fahad Al-Hashmi/Barkat Al-Sharji (OMA) 6-1 6-3

30 March

Syria v Jordan, Tajikistan v Brunei, United Arab Emirates v Oman – not played due to rain

Final Positions: 1. Syria, 2. Tajikistan, 3. United Arab Emirates, 4. Oman, 5. Brunei, 6. Jordan

American Group
May 1–3, Southampton, Bermuda

May 1

Bermuda defeated Costa Rica 2-1
Ricky Mallory (BER) d. Fernando Martinez (CRC) 6-3 7-5
Donald Evans (BER) d. Federico Camacho (CRC) 2-6 7-6(2) 6-4
Javier Solera/Marin Echandi (CRC) d. Michael Way/James Collieson (BER) 7-6(2) 3-6 6-4

May 2

Costa Rica defeated OECS 2-1
Glynn James (ECA) d. Jaiver Solera (CRC) 6-2 6-4
Federico Camacho (CRC) d. Vernon Lewis (ECA) 0-6 7-5 6-3
Fernando Martinez/Martin Echandi (CRC) d. Glynn James/Gary Eugene (ECA) 7-5 13 Ret.

May 3

Bermuda defeated OECS 2-1
James Collieson (BER) d. Gary Eugene (ECA) 6-2 6-2
Vernon Lewis (ECA) d. Donald Evans (BER) 6-2 6-2
Ricky Mallory/Michael Way (BER) d. Vernon Lewis/Gary Eugene (ECA) 7-5 7-6(4)

Final Positions: 1. Bermuda, 2. Costa Rica, 3. OECS

World Group: The Road to the Championship

First Round February 7–9	Quarterfinal Round April 4–6	Semifinal Round September 19–21	Final Round November 28–30	Champion Nation
USA	USA 4-1	USA 4-1	USA 4-1	
Brazil				
Netherlands	Netherlands 3-2			
Romania				
Australia	Australia 4-1	Australia 5-0		
France				
Czech Republic	Czech Republic 3-2			Sweden 5-0
India				
Italy	Italy 4-1	Italy 4-1		
Mexico				
Spain	Spain 4-1		Sweden 4-1	
Germany				
South Africa	South Africa 3-1	Sweden 3-2		
Russia				
Sweden	Sweden 4-1			
Switzerland				

Acknowledgments

During the months it took to prepare this book, numerous people in the small world of men's tennis generously shared their time and thoughts with me. I would like to express my special thanks to the following captains, coaches and players: Harivony Andrianafetra, Paolo Bertolucci, Jonas Björkman, Wayne Black, Omar Camporese, Sergio Cruz, Jim Courier, Stefan Edberg, John Fitzgerald, Stanley Franker, Tom Gullikson, Carl-Axel Hageskog, Anders Jarryd, John Kasule, Gustavo Kuerten, Jean-Komi Loglo, Todd Martin, John Newcombe, Yannick Noah, Patrick Rafter, Tony Roche, Pete Sampras, Einar Sigurgeirsson, Oli Sveinsson, Todd Woodbridge and Mark Woodforde.

I also would like to thank Neil Amdur, Nicola Arzani, Peter Bengtsson, Peter Berlin, Page Crosland, Donna Doherty, Jane Fraser, Alun James, Thomas Hallberg, Margaret Heenan, Jay Jennings, Doug MacCurdy, Jorge Salkeld, Ubaldo Scanagatta, Wolfgang Schadler, Claus Stauder, Fred Stolle, Christopher Stokes, Euphemia Tlhapane, Alan Trengove, Randy Walker, Kelly Wolf and the reporters at L'Equipe, particularly Philippe Bouin, whom I consider the world's finest tennis writer. Biggest thanks go to Alexandra Tart, Barbara Travers and Derek Ungless for putting up with my hectic schedule amidst their own, and above all, to my wife, Virginie, who puts up with my hectic schedule year in and year out.

Christopher Clarey

Photography Credits